MW01089943

Automated Journalism at the Intersection of Politics and Black Culture

The Battle against Digital Hegemony

Colin H. Campbell

LEXINGTON BOOKS
Lanham • Boulder • New York • London

Published by Lexington Books
An imprint of The Rowman & Littlefield Publishing Group, Inc.
4501 Forbes Boulevard, Suite 200, Lanham, Maryland 20706
www.rowman.com

86-90 Paul Street, London EC2A 4NE, United Kingdom

British Library Cataloguing in Publication Information Available

Library of Congress Cataloging-in-Publication Data

Names: Campbell, Colin H., 1971–author.
Title: Automated journalism at theintersection of politics and Black culture: the battle
    against digital hegemony / Colin Campbell.
Description: Lanham: LexingtonBooks, 2024. | Includes bibliographical references and
    index.
Summary: "This book delivers a critical look at the social and racial costs of relying
    on artificial intelligence to produce journalism without human controls in editorial
    expression, equity, and accuracy"— Provided by publisher.
Identifiers: LCCN 2023049547(print) | LCCN 2023049548 (ebook) |
    ISBN 9781666913330 (cloth) | ISBN 9781666913347 (epub)
Subjects: LCSH: Online journalism—UnitedStates. | Artificial intelligence. |
    African Americans—Press coverage. | Minorities—Press coverage—United States. |
    Journalism—Objectivity—United States. | Multimedia data mining.
Classification: LCC PN4784.O62 C3652024 (print) | LCC PN4784.O62 (ebook) |
    DDC 071/.3—dc23/eng/20231113
LC record available at https://lccn.loc.gov/2023049547
LC ebook record available at https://lccn.loc.gov/2023049548

Tomy family: my parents, Floyd and Janyce; my siblings, Chrystal and Courtney;and all my loved ones for their continued love and support while pushing me tostrive, achieve, and succeed

Automated Journalism at the Intersection of Politics and Black Culture

Contents

List of Figures

Chapter 1

Technological Determinism in the Age of Artificial Intelligence

We are living in an exciting time to witness significant communications advancements. Digital capabilities broadened by the internet and programmable platforms using the latest technologies are creating greater opportunities within our journalistic institutions. The progressive combination of these areas creates wider spaces to explore their synergies expressed through digital journalism, which is being recognized as the most modern form of news gathering and reporting.

Editorial content created in the digital journalism space is often collected from varied sources and then disseminated via the internet. This means of production differs from conventional methods that have included in-person interviewing and consequent publishing in print or broadcasting through television or radio platforms. These distinctions are necessary to acknowledge because the media landscape is changing. Reporters have conventionally used Electronic News Gathering (ENG) techniques to gather and present news.

Digital news gathering (DNG) is the evolution; the more contemporary form of information collecting and reporting systems (Sterling, 2009). The term "digital news gathering" is often synonymously used with ENG. However, conflating these terms creates a misunderstanding. Digital media platforms and comparative digital journalism have evolved, but they are also depending more on content found online through the world wide web. The research supported in this book would be more accurately described as DNG, advanced DNG, or augmented DNG because the reporting methods discussed here take conventional and ENG forms of news gathering and information collection and amplify their speed, content, and public reach through collated internet material. This amplification, of course, would not be possible without constant diligence in developing technological advancements that allow for web scraping and other agglomeration strategies.

Americans and their compatriots in the West are becoming more active in their engagement of internet materials. The ubiquity of electronic and digital devices providing media that consumers read on smartphones, tablets, laptops, computers, and other computer-related accoutrements expands every year. Mobile technologies and their increasingly mundane influences are concatenate to progressive computing abilities and connectivity. Technology has been and still is considered an engine of global development, with internet-related technological advances contributing significantly to net-positive economic variability. There is little question that the desire to receive news from myriad sources has profoundly impacted how we receive information and view the world around us. The ease of access to various sourcing materials decreases the need to purchase numerous newspapers, magazines, and other tangible media when essentially the same volume of information can be accessed from the palms of our hands through smart phones, phablets, tablets, and other digital accoutrements.

At the same time, societies are adapting their reading habits. Media corporations are researching and implementing methods to optimize production and augment their readerships. One of the areas where companies are continuing to develop technologies is through using algorithms to create news and information content otherwise known as "automated journalism."

News companies are already using automated journalism in various capacities. By applying artificial intelligence (AI) software supported by machine learning and Natural Language Processing (NLP), most story content is manufactured by computers, if not totally by a computer. The algorithmic production process takes already existing data sets, analyzes the information, and then converts the data into readable narratives that are eventually reviewed by humans to confirm grammatical and syntactic integrity as well as accuracy.

Newsrooms are using machine learning, an advanced computational process, to evaluate and collate massive amounts of data. This is where machines perform algorithmic computations without always needing direct intervention. The process is directed by a series of algorithms controlled by computation. This same expeditious process, unassisted by humans, would take numerous people an exponential amount of time to reproduce identical material within a similar timeframe. That process amid a digital age is more common than the average media consumer may think. Going back to 2012, news leaders in the media industry have already been testing and deploying algorithms in software redesigns for their newsrooms.

The developing technology allows for huge advancements in newsroom proficiency and accomplishment. However, concerns are being raised about the use of the technology, especially as it pertains to individuals, groups, or populations that have been traditionally excluded from the news-gathering process and its subsequent narrative output. The problematization is augmented when certain people have been inaccurately or unfairly repre-sented. For this reason, automated journalism, a form of digital journalism, has become a main topic within discussions of ethical AI concomitant with pre-emptive algorithmic justice considerations.

When we look at the history of United States media, we observe that there are patterns of revisionist history. From the historical inaccuracies of Chris-topher Columbus and colonizing Europeans to the portrayals of enslaved Africans commonly called "slaves" in American parlance and their placement in US history, we can aver that racism and the power dynamics associated with a cultural hierarchy are present throughout our media. This, of course, creates another set of issues when tracking the epistemological foundations that contribute to the understanding of our world. Even today, many Ameri-cans believe that the Civil War was purely about states' rights precluding the understanding that the war was for some Americans to preserve the system of chattel slavery that placed Black Americans in bondage to later be considered and treated as subhuman (Devlin, 2023).

There have been movements to counter prevailing unbalanced narratives, however. The importance of the Black press to expose and amend white-washed, sanitized narratives has always occupied space in US history. As US colonists fought against the British, the stories of Black soldiers could be found in alternative media. As newspapers covered the Civil War and discussed western expansion, scattered participants of the Black press wrote about the future of emancipation, Jim Crow, and the lynchings of Black Americans rooted in domestic terrorism.

Nearly two centuries later, members of Black media continue to advocate for social equality, equity, and for Black society to become better civic stew-ards. Within this activism, community leaders push back against restrictions to voting access, health inequalities, education disparities, and systemic racism within US institutions. The most vociferous voices targeting these matters often come from members of Black media. If they are not coming directly from members of the press, Black reporters are amplifying the voices of individuals who speak to these issues. Even in the wake of George Floyd's murder in May 2020, white-owned companies representing mainstream and legacy media were not as persistent and outspoken regarding his murder as Black media had been. The disproportionate lack of attention addressing the importance of the situation-based context was entangled with other issues and became politically diluted like so many other social challenges facing Black society, such as the Black/white wealth disparity, mass incarceration, or political participation. For example, for many white Americans, stories regarding cash bail and pretrial detentions resulting in economic and racial inequalities do not reach the level of existential concern that they would in Black society.

Black media is also more likely to report on issues regarding Africa and other countries within the African diaspora (including the Caribbean) more than mainstream media. Black media often centers the humanity of people who are very often dehumanized by the predominate white society creating the structures of operation that influence the masses. Black media often pays more attention to people killed by police brutality including the victims' family members. That cultural connection of empathy could be traced back to the origins of America's Black Press, which throughout history has usually only been highlighted in academia outside of the mainstream specter that most of US society observes and that digitally algorithmic narratives take their cues from.

This book is about the caveats of augmented journalism using Artificial Intelligence (AI) technologies and the use of algorithms in journalism, especially as it pertains to information regarding Black society. When analyzing the potential effects of this powerful technology, it broadens the case to argue for the need of ethical AI. At the intersection of technology, culture, news, and media sit relationships that could perpetuate what I describe as *digital hegemony*, a sociocultural, socioeconomic, or ideological dominance exerted through technological extension.In some ways, it could be considered as a hyponym to techno hegemony. As we rely on the use of algorithms on digital platforms, there is a need to be cognizant of consequential limitations and ramifications. For example, ChatGPT, an artificial intelligence chatbot, combining the names "chat" and "Generative Pre-trained Transformer," has rocketed to popularity in recent years because of its ability to deliver customized information using large language models and language processing backed by programmed algorithms (Sun, 2022). However, this technology was not the first to deliver performance indicators related to big data expression in newsgathering functions.

This volume discusses why it is paramount to be proper stewards of artificial intelligence technologies in journalism, especially when being cognizant of issues of race in a western context. As a researcher, I have also studied cultural issues and events in the US, particularly when it comes to the experience of Blackness. AI systems and technologies are being used in crucial areas of our society more and more, such as criminal justice, hiring and lending, healthcare, and more. Biased outcomes have the potential to have a significant impact on societies, communities, and individuals. Improper application of AI technologies could exacerbate and sustain historical injustices that Black populations in the US are still suffering from, such as wealth inequality and overrepresented populations in the country's prison populations (Aladangady & Forde, 2021).

When looking at the use of emerging technologies in journalism, it is also important to look at transparency and accountability. When factoring in racial implications, it helps to boost accountability in AI systems. By identifying and understanding biased sources, we are better able to make progress in designing improved algorithms and models. The result would be improved literacy discernment, better auditing, enhanced bias mitigation, and evaluating outputs. Being consistent in these areas would bolster trust and accountability in news-writing AI and its capabilities.

Algorithms play a large and influential role in how we receive information through the internet, but with these innocuously intended machinations come the caveats of how these information-delivering algorithms are programmed. This also applies to AI. As a researcher who is sensitive to the aims of social equity, I realize that there must be an observation of how the utilization of these technologies could worsen societal divisions or inequalities if left unmonitored and subsequently amended. By providing some historical context and successive developments in media, this manuscript will help to elucidate how AI and algorithms in news production and the interpretations of their conveyance could proliferate misinformation and, even worse, disinformation in news by promoting information silos, entrenching selective biases, and exacerbating digital hegemony in the expansion of technological determinism.

Chapter 2

Algorithmic Beginnings

Since the first academic conference in 1956, called the Dartmouth Summer Research Project on Artificial Intelligence, the use of processes and calculations in machines to simulate human thinking has increasingly gained global attention for its potential use in various industries. Recently, this interest has expanded to communications and journalism called "automated journalism," although terms such as augmented journalism, robot-assisted journalism, and even machine-assisted journalism have also been used.

Automated journalism is the product of a specific form of artificial intelligence (AI) and algorithm synergy that generates news articles to be reviewed by humans before final publishing. The purpose of this study is to understand how news is presented using this process with regard to Black Americans and events that have a direct impact on them. This research examines the framing of Black politicians and racialized events from a company that has specialized in the use of automated journalism to create online news reports. Moreover, this analysis compares this framing to news reports from more conventional online media sources.

Agenda setting theory and framing theory served as the theoretical foundation for this research because, according to McCombs et al. (2013), media shape and determine what issues are important in the minds of the public. According to Goffman (1974), framing is at the core of news content to provide context to the presented information. Much of what automated journalism collates during production has already reached a level of news salience.

A framing analysis and a thematic analysis were conducted to scrutinize each domain of online news media for their final comparison. This research included an examination of white-owned/mainstream online media, Black-centric media that focuses on news and information from a Black American

7

perspective, and an automated journalism source across nearly 300 online news articles during the 2018 US midterm election season.

This research connected and compared narrative expressions between the white-owned and mainstream media sources, the Blackcentric media sources, and the automated journalism source in framing Black American politicians and racialized events. Framing is an essential part of message conveyance. Proper framing can decrease the obfuscation of esoteric contextualization by cohesively presenting the information in a way that the content consumers can understand. Framing allows for a perceived reality to be more noticeable and at times more relatable. The downside of framing is that it is often subjective, allowing for manufactured biases to creep in.

This study contributes to emerging empirical work regarding the impact of framing derived from the inchoate system of automated journalism at the intersection of culture and politics. The research also raises awareness of necessary considerations to support ethical AI in communications and journalism.

THE ISSUES FACING ETHICAL ARTIFICIAL INTELLIGENCE (AI)

Truth and accuracy in media matter, and greater numbers of Americans are looking to digital media sources for information. According to recent polling, 86 percent of Americans report getting their news online from the internet, more than double the amount of people who receive information from television alone (Jerome, Hie, Hadzmy, et al., 2023; Gottfried & Shearer, 2017). Developments in technology and computer programming have led to a rise in artificial intelligence (AI) and use of algorithms in development of news narratives described as automated journalism (Graefe, 2016). Automated journalism is "the process of using software or algorithms to automatically generate news stories without human intervention—after the initial programming of the algorithm" (Graefe, 2016, 11). Andreas Graefe, an academician known for his *Guide to Automated Journalism* (2016), discusses the future trajectory of automated journalism with assistance from AI technologies and algorithmic expression. He and other academicians describe how algorithms driven by a specific form of AI software can create thousands of news stories on an individual topic more quickly, more cheaply, and with fewer errors than a human (Carlson, 2015; Graefe, 2016). Of course, the realization of these computer-enabled capabilities has created a panic among journalists based on the fear that automated content production in journalism could replace them (Carlson, 2015). This research discusses why computers, although widely applicable, are still a distance away from supplanting human engagement in the development of journalistic content.

AI is the science of operating machines to process options and make decisions similarly to humans. An algorithm uses some inputs of information or data and uses mathematics combined with logic to produce an output of information. Artificial intelligence algorithms are a combination of both concepts. AI algorithms use inputs and outputs simultaneously to facilitate the learning of the data to produce an output when given new input data and/or information. AI is, in essence, a vast area of computer science that is focused on building and utilizing machines that are capable of performing tasks that usually require human brain thinking and processing to accomplish. Algorithms are small pieces of code that tell a computer how to accomplish a specific task. They tell the computer what to do in order to produce a certain objective. Think of an algorithm as a recipe on how to bake a batch of vegan cookies. The AI component would represent a human's thinking process about how to craft the recipe and adapt the recipe for the intended palate. Together, AI algorithms are a synergy of processing power and capability with a programmed method of how to perform a certain task. If one were to compare the synergy of AI algorithmic computation to a car and driver, the AI would be the human manipulating all the parts of the car, which would be the algorithms, to get to a desired destination. "The key difference is that an algorithm defines the process through which a decision is made, and AI uses training data to make such a decision" (Mousavi as cited in Ismail, 2018, 1).

AI allows computers to think and learn. Despite its presence since the 1950s, it is only now starting to be widely applied to other industries, including communications and journalism, as computer chips augment computational power. According to research firm Markets and Markets, the AI market is expected to grow at about 37 percent each year and reach $191 billion by 2025.

Carlson (2015), a well-known researcher in the field of AI use in journalism, described algorithmic use guided by AI as "processes that convert data into narrative news texts with limited to no human intervention beyond the initial programming choices" (416–31). The conversion happens in real time, indicating the potential to exceed conventional news journalism production.

Algorithms and artificial intelligence are making decisions for people and organizations. This new reality promises increased productivity, efficient use of resources, and enhanced business development. However, AI algorithm technologies can, at their worst, support encoded biases, leading to discrimination, learned helplessness, and even fatalities (so far, in affairs outside of communications). Ignoring racial implications in AI biases could encourage further discrimination against populations using their race or ethnic background as a metric to substantiate bigotry or social chauvinism. Coming to terms with these implications is vital for comprehensive acknowledgment and awareness to avoid discriminatory behaviors in AI systems.

Automated journalism is occurring as many newsroom directors maintain that computer assistance when using a specific form of AI and algorithms that could augment a reporter's efforts in the field (Carlson, 2015). This research examines the news purveyor Knowhere, which uses algorithms to remove biases from published news narratives. However, as this research suggests and as social scientists have contended, algorithms have their limitations and cannot perform the same interrogation and contextualization that humans can (Levendowski, 2018). Scholars are studying the effects of this technology in terms of copyrighting, ethics, representation, and more (Carlson, 2015; Graefe, 2016; Weeks, 2014).

Creators at the digital journalism news company Knowhere have looked at the limitations and insularity that many media consumers build when looking for news that resonates with their interests. For example, the Pew Research Center estimated that 45 percent of people and rising get their news from Facebook (Gesenhues, 2017). Facebook has recently admitted that their news and information is curated by an algorithm that caters to individual users' tastes (Constine, 2019). This means that news that might contradict a user's point of view may not be introduced to a user, resulting in a one-sided perspective in their understanding of news and events. This is a form of narrowcasting in the digital space. This type of targeted or niche marketing involves aiming media messaging at certain segments of society, regulated by a variety of individual preferences, values, or demographic affiliations. Narrowcasting is growing in popularity, mainly because it is a departure from the convention of broadcasting to a large audience simultaneously. Narrowcasting offers more individual and non-temporally restrictive access to information, with a postmodern concept in mind that mass audiences in the traditional sense of consuming content are on the decline. It is noticeable that the proliferate use of social media and the convergence between electronic and digital spaces is blurring the line between what is considered to be narrowcast and broadcast.

Knowhere creators endeavored to write the "most unbiased news on the planet" (Elkrief, 2019). Editorial decisions are made based on the data that the curators (editors) receive from an internet systemization process. Using a specific type of AI, the quantity of information that is published about a given story informs a score that is then ranked as part of a prioritization process. From there, Knowhere editors are directed to select stories to cover that day. Stories that are similar in scope are categorized together and scrutinized by the AI program. Algorithms draft a story from that cluster of similar information. This process happens numerous times, collating various stories of interest. The series of clusters are constantly re-evaluated, and the prioritization cue is constantly modified based on dominant story narratives throughout the day. Once the collected information from the internet exhibits a salient event cluster, a human journalist or editor picks the story for the AI-powered system to build a story. The system chooses facts from the information mined from the internet. The process continues by writing the story based on the collected news narratives. Knowhere's stories were often split into three parts—left, right, and neutral—to reflect partisan biases in the narrative.

Automated journalism advocates state that the technology has the ability to streamline workflows, automate mundane tasks, crunch more data than humans, dig out media insights, diminish the presence of fake or misleading news, generate publishable narratives, and overall augment a journalist's capabilities (Underwood, 2019). Computerized content can deliver news more quickly than humans can. Looking at this list of supposed benefits, the emerging technology of algorithm-driven and -produced news content is fascinating because of its potential for efficiency. However, those who study algorithms and their synergy with human civilization already know about some of the technology's shortcomings. Researchers have indicated the pernicious effects of systematic and repeatable anomalies in computer systems that generate unfair outcomes, such as privileging one group of users over others driven by algorithmic bias. This algorithmic bias is not isolated to text information. Whether algorithms in self-driving cars tend to see white pedestrians on the street more than darker-complexioned people or questionable results appear after a search query on the internet, such as those reported in Dr. Safiya Noble's book *Algorithms of Oppression* (2018); there are serious concerns regarding how algorithms are used for the alleged benefit of society.

Computer programmers and the critics of their work are sensitive to what is often referred to as garbage in, garbage out (GIGO). This anomaly occurs when flawed or erroneous information is input into a computer process resulting in the output of the regurgitated information (Pederson, R., Kalita, B., & Burke, K., 2022, 357–358). GIGO is also referenced when there is a deficit in programmers' decision-making because of faulty, insufficient, or inaccurate data. Reckless programming that feeds models inferior data leads to impractical results that do not encourage confidence in the information. Without being mindful of GIGO, it is impossible to design a system that works the way it should be intended. An initially flawed system will result in a waste of resources and money. Rubbish in, rubbish out (RIRO) is also used to express the concept (Adair, J. 2009).

Further concerns are raised when the misdirected practice affects black box AI results. This happens when inputs and operations are not clear to users or anyone examining outcomes. The black–white binary distinction has often been conflated with the categorization of good and evil. Much like other terms in American English nomenclature, the preceding word, "black," denotes a negative connotation similar to a blacklist, a list of items such as IP addresses or websites that are considered undesirable and pernicious; or black hat hackers, who are described as criminals who break into computer networks with malicious intent (Porterfield, 2016, 37). The massive amount of processing needed for machine learning sifts through billions of data points to resolve issues and answer queries, but how the program arrives at its conclusions is not always made clear. And it is increasingly noticeable how these programs can develop biases and stereotypes without us realizing why or how it is happening.

On February 23, 2018, the Knight Media Forum, a national organization that focuses on media equity and participation to promote a healthy democracy, held its annual conference. The conference theme was "Strengthening Local News, Community and Democracy" (Prince, 2018). The conference featured a cadre of librarians, members of community foundations, and journalists. This group noted the urgency of addressing trust, media, and democracy, especially when dealing with communities of color and how they are framed in the media.

Amy Webb, futurist, author, and founder of the "Future Today Institute," discussed the use of current technologies such as AI and algorithms to create news stories. When asked about the future for communities of color in the face of the increasing production of advanced technologies, Webb delivered a less than optimistic view and said that that future did not look good (Prince, 2018). Webb explained that any member of a community who has felt invisible could feel further isolated by technologies that do not recognize cultural impacts (Prince, 2018).

Webb is the author of "The Signals Are Talking: Why Today's Fringe Is Tomorrow's Mainstream: Forecast and Take Action on Tomorrow's Trends, Today" (Webb, 2016). Webb challenged current conditions in journalism regarding the implementation of algorithms for news narratives. Webb noted that, since the beginning of computing, "big data" and algorithms have leaked into nearly every aspect of media communications, from social interactions to economics (Alcorn, 2018). Few of us are surprised when we call a number and the initial response on the other end is a digitally synthesized voice.

New data systems and technologies could improve messaging access for Black Americans and communities of color. Conversely, if the technology is not controlled, it could be destructive to those marginalized communities. Webb stated that, without proper oversight, Black society at large would have less control over the framing of race or other pertinent issues. As Webb and other panelists have indicated, discrimination could be a high-tech, high-stakes enterprise (Prince, 2018).

A *New York Times* article entitled "Artificial Intelligence's White Guy Problem" warned about the dangerous impacts of AI when bias is factored in. "Sexism, racism, and other forms of discrimination are being built into the machine-learning algorithms that underlie the technology behind many 'intelligent' systems that shape how we are categorized and advertised to" (Crawford, 2016, SR11).

The implications of neglect when observing the use of algorithms are concerning. *The Guardian*, a British daily newspaper, reported on the potential of training of AI in algorithm-driven journalism "how to be prejudiced" (Sanchez, 2017). Science journalist Dana Sanchez wrote that, as machines approach levels of task-based objectives combined with language understanding ability similar to that of humans, they are assimilating inherent biases in language patterns (Sanchez, 2017). These biases could skew how society interprets news and information. Sanchez posited that algorithms are not biased automatically; rather, people are biased, and AI-controlled algorithm-driven information is including those inherent biases.

The permanence of internet information threatens to preserve information discrimination and prejudice for generations if left unobserved and unaddressed. Biases that may be embedded in data could become entrenched in the logic of everyday algorithmic systems that go on to develop biased data pieces (Montal & Reich, 2017).

There are further implications that algorithm-driven and algorithm-generated data deriving from unregulated mainstream media could have a detrimental impact on society. Crawford (2016) posited that, ultimately, the potential problems associated with AI applications could be avoided by applying proper attention and diligence. "This is fundamentally a data problem. Algorithms learn by being fed certain images, often chosen by engineers" (Crawford, 2016, p. 1). Critical thinking skills are necessary to reduce or eliminate automation biases.

This research focuses on a specific area of systematic industry where artificial intelligence (AI) technologies, online news journalism, and (Black) sociopolitical culture intersect. The work emphasized here also examines the interplay within the Black experience, journalism, and technology. Many of the explored areas within this literature look specifically at the "Blackcentric" experience in 2018, when news production was focused on political news.

Chapter 3

Understanding Automated Journalism

As briefly described before, the terms *automated journalism, robot journalism, AI in journalism, algorithmic journalism, algorithmically-based journalism, automated robot journalism, robo-journalism,* and occasionally, *augmented journalism* have all been used to describe the increasing practice of using programmed computer-based technologies to create news narratives as we as a society try to better understand how the technology is evolving (Broussard, 2015; Carlson, 2015; Graef, 2016; Latar, 2018). These various terms reflect that the technology and how it is implemented are being understood and accepted slowly.

This study uses the term *automated journalism,* the word *algorithm,* and its lexical derivatives. Scholars, with the assistance of industry experts, have sought to understand the narrow artificially intelligent task of scouring the internet for data and then producing news articles with blazing speeds, understanding that this action is a subset of artificial intelligence programming for a focused task (Montal & Reich, 2016).

Through use of AI driven by computer software, news narratives are created largely through a type of computerized technological production instead of human labor such as general assignment news reporters. The use of this technological production is described as an "expert system" (Broussard, 2015). An expert system is very data dependent. For an expert system to create a logical path for a desired output, data are needed as an input to initiate and control the paths, such as a set of parameters that the algorithm is expected to follow. Algorithm-driven operations directed by AI interpret and present the data in a readable format for human consumption (Graefe, 2016). Very often, the process of aggregating digital content to be rendered as news narratives incorporates an algorithm that scours large amounts of data to create a variety of predetermined article formats, such as length, focus, and details about an event or person (Carlson, 2015; Graefe, 2016). This process of creating news requires minimal human involvement, but as Graefe (2016) noted, it is still necessary to provide overall comprehensive assimilation.

Automated journalism is being developed to remove "heavy lifting" from the journalistic production process, from selecting content to report on to distribution. The implications in this area are vast. Artificial Intelligence can be programmed to generate news articles of varying narratives. This process works in seconds. There is a potential here to save editors' and reporters' time in the newsroom. A platform of this type of speed and power could also save large costs for news organizations. However, communications scholars are expressing some reservations, including narrative quality, editorial neutrality, and the potential of industry-wide job losses. AI has been used to personalize news and has enormous implications for how consumers receive news. Journalistic expression could be modified based on the preferences of the consumer. As the technology evolves, it is becoming more popular in newsrooms. But with the increased popularity comes concerns about information exclusion or unintended biases (Graefe, 2016). Automated journalism categorizes news articles that are generated by computer programs. Using algorithms powered by AI software, these stories are produced largely without human intervention. These programs interpret, categorize, and introduce data in a readable format for human consumption. This type of data delivery is based on an algorithm that analyzes large amounts of information, restructures the information, determines salient points, and replaces details, including names, places, amounts, rankings, statistics, and other figures. This data assimilation can be customized to a specific voice, intention, or style.

Because the algorithmic process to generate news can be complex, there may be unpredictable risks (Russell & Norvig, 2016). Associated risks have generated questions such as: Could some stories be overlooked because of subtle linguistic nuances in vocabulary between Black and white communities through neural natural language processing? Could there be neglect of a particular story because it does not fit specific narratives within the mainstream white community? Could some stories be ignored because they stem from communities that are not expected to buy the content or publication being produced? Could a person's character be besmirched under a skewed view because access to the dominant narrative is disproportionately unbalanced? Many of these questions and more are valid when examining this emerging mode of journalistic production. If there are discrepancies, there could be an undefinable social cost in terms of obscuring comprehensive understanding of issues. Consistent engagement in skewed or biased news augments selective biases and traps consumers in communication silos. With an abundance of information proliferating in digital spaces, the need for fact-checking and verification will become more important. Of course, precise fact-checking is easier in quantitative ways rather than in interpretations that are qualitative and nuanced in determination. This could lead to errors in accuracy and nuanced interpretation.

The use of AI in journalism also raises concerns over accountability, bias, and privacy. There are concerns about the use of personal information and data to customize news delivery. The potential for biases in AI algorithms that are used to create and curate content have the potential to disenfranchise certain populations. This study is concerned with the potential hazard of reducing or restricting news that could have a deleterious impact on society because of information disseminated through the increasing use of automated content development methods.

As Lewis et al. (2019) indicated, "A key aspect in this process is the rise of automated forms of journalism, such as stories produced not by human authors but written by machines" (62). The resulting articles can be tailored for various styles, including tone or voice (Graefe, 2016). "Robotic reporter" scholar Matt Carlson (2015) described the young field of automated journalism as "algorithmic processes that convert data into narrative news texts with limited to no human intervention beyond the initial programming" (417).

Carlson (2018) wrote that the journalistic process is in a constant battle. He noted that deference to the goals of objectivity and the popularity of news production leave little space for subjectivity of journalistic choice. Because of these demands for accuracy and expediency in journalism, anxieties over the increased use of algorithmic journalism in automated production is growing. Carlson posited that algorithmic judgment should be considered separately from the professional discretion of a professional journalist. He argued that sedulous algorithmic judgment creates challenges based on beliefs that human subjectivity can be whimsical and should be supplanted with a more consistent process. Algorithms are designed to be as objective as possible, albeit subject to implementation preferences of the controller. Carlson (2018) noted that algorithmic judgment produces a profound impact on news and any discourse that is involved in its creation. Carlson (2015) did not go into detail about the results of omitting perspectives of subaltern groups living within a co-cultural existence. Carlson could have produced a more provocative study by underlining the need for attention to diversity in the monitoring and application of automated journalism. Such matters are being touched upon here.

Waddell (2019), writing that using the Modality-Agency-Interactivity-Navigability (MAIN) model as a framework to understand human relationships based on news produced by nonhuman actors, noted "audiences are less likely to perceive news attributed to machines as biased" because they perceive machines to be "less subjective" (83). However, Waddell did not look at the inductive framing of issues created by algorithm-generated content or how the process could affect narratives dealing with sensitive issues such as race or biases created by exclusion of information. The current study examines the dynamics of biases and racial implications achieved through automated journalistic means.

Experts and scholars have posted the caveats about employing automated journalistic production (Dörr, 2016). Some see it as a benefit because it can allow journalists more time to research other parts of a story or to carry out more complex tasks (referred to as "augmented"; Carlson, 2015). For example, where automated journalism has been used to report sports stories, "the automated stories reportedly contained far fewer errors than those written by humans" (DeJarnette, 2016). In other areas of the media and journalism industries, the use of automated journalism could cut costs and time (Dörr, 2016). The refutation of such ostensible efficiencies created through artificial intelligence could be offered in neuroscientists' views of haste in productivity. Richard Heitz, a neuroscientist at Vanderbilt University, discovered that when we, as humans, try to do things too fast, we make more errors. Many could argue that a computer system mimicking the human mind would be subject to similar failings. This does not mean the interest in AI developing technologies is on the brink of being stifled. In fact, it is just the opposite. The utility of automated journalism is expected to increase in a similar way as other communication technologies where "advances in product and process technology have caused disruptions in industry structure by changing the status quo of the competitive landscape" (Onwumechili, 2017, 181).

However, automated journalism is seen as a potential threat to the ownership and job prospects of news reporters (Dörr, 2016). There are relatively few studies examining automated journalism in comparison to other areas involved in mass media effects. Hanson et al. (2017) looked at AI in the newsroom regarding how it is used and how it operates. Researchers worked with other digital journalists and the Brown Institute for Media Innovation and assembled a policy reform forum of technologists and journalists to understand how AI could be adapted into the journalism industry. Using a case study method, the researchers came to this conclusion:

> There needs to be a concerted and continued effort to fight hidden bias in AI, often unacknowledged but always present, since tools are programmed by humans. Journalists must strive to insert transparency into their stories, noting in familiar and non-technical terms how AI was used to help their reporting or production. (Hansen et al., 2017, 3)

In a media industry driven by evolving changes concomitant with technology, journalism is being transformed. The use of new tools and insights is reforming the ways in which news is navigated, produced, disseminated, and consumed. The world is experiencing the emergence of new technologies and customs, a dynamic that involves new methods to produce news and modifying the journalistic environment. Despite fears of the deleterious potential in the latest trends for the quality of journalism and employment sustainability, some developments are clearing the way to a journalism industry paradigm. But how these changes disturb the status quo could change just as rapidly as the technologies that are designed to support it.

One of the major areas where algorithmically generated content is being scrutinized is how automated journalism builds narratives by assembling "texts, images, spectacles, events, and cultural artifacts that tell a story" (The Royal Society, 2018). How a story is told can improve or restrict the potential for human development. The study of these narratives is important to understand their function and engage with them discerningly. There could also be a need for re-examining newsworthiness and the attributions the public places on media's influence, skewed by self-serving biases. These biases encourage tendencies to connect our positive personal perspectives to our own lived experiences while attributing failures to external factors orchestrated by uncontrollable situational circumstances. By way of psychological egoism, it is part of human nature to react positively to successful factors that we, ourselves, experience through our own volition and negatively respond to scenarios that we can blame on others if they do not work to our advantage or support our world view.

UNDERSTANDING ALGORITHMS

Algorithms are present in all aspects of computer-adjacent living, including digital forms of communication. Algorithms can be considered as a piece of code. This code tells a computer how to achieve a certain task (Russell & Norvig, 2016). In many ways, an algorithm is like a recipe for an end product for public consumption. For example, one who uses Google or Facebook or a car's global positioning satellite (GPS) device is engaging with an algorithm (Xue et al., 2010). Algorithms are basically sets of instructions or calculations for a computer. Results can be aggregated and used to orchestrate how certain programs are executed.

Algorithms perform many important tasks and decisions in daily life. People place implicit confidence in algorithms to plan travel, to navigate materials to read, and to participate in the world of social media (Bucher, 2017, p. 30). Algorithms affect how people understand the world inside and outside of the digital space. They are doing this more autonomously than in the past due to technological advancements (Bucher, 2017, p. 33).

At the beginning of the millennium (2000), computer algorithms operated by following a specific set of commands or instructions created by computer programmers. Nearly twenty years later, algorithms are more advanced. More current and updated algorithms teach themselves (Graefe, 2016).

Instead of relying on a step-by-step list of predetermined and programmed instructions designed by computer engineers, algorithms now use a system of operations called "machine learning," an application of artificial intelligence that employs a system of computers called "neural networks" and vast amounts of data to make decisions. The objective of machine learning is to create a system of computer-based operations and functions in which a machine can learn without being explicitly programmed (Rubaai, Ricketts, & Kankam, 2002, p. 441). In many ways, present-day algorithms are "self-taught" to form their own code to address new functions, including the discovery of answers to questions and new information. These sets of self-taught algorithms are being used increasingly in journalism as part of an automated journalism format that is expected to grow in efficiency and use (Graefe, 2016).

Algorithms that are driven by a form of artificial intelligence have slowly entered nearly all areas of media platforms. These algorithmic programs are responsible for collecting information, writing content, distributing content, and collecting responses to the content (Dartnall, 2013). These programs can interpret, organize, categorize, and present data in ways that a human can read in an agreeable format. These consumable formats have found their way into journalism and media. Most commonly, the process involves an algorithm that scans copious amounts of data, selects from a variety of preprogrammed article structures, looks for key points, and inserts necessary details such as nouns, people, places, and things to round out the news story.

The news media website Knowhere works by searching the internet for trending news stories. The vision that inspired the leaders of the California-based company has been to take journalism from an AI-adjacent industry into an AI-driven industry. Knowhere's creators contend that AI can remove bias from the news that it aggregates. Knowhere's proprietary algorithm sorts and categorizes the newest published articles from the internet, in almost real time, to determine what news stories are being reported by news sites on the internet (A. Elkrief, personal communication, July 3, 2019). The website *Crunchbase* describes Knowhere as follows:

> Knowhere is a news company that claims to be the most unbiased news source available on the web. The purpose of Knowhere news is to enhance social discourse by providing high-quality, unbiased news and by arming readers with the tools to see all sides of a story. They practice journalism differently, harnessing the collective intelligence of the web in order to write the world's most objective news stories on the events shaping the world. They believe the collaboration of journalists with machine learning tools is the only path to a truly global and

impartial home of news. Hearing every voice, writing without agenda, in search of the truth. (Crunchbase, 2019, 1)

After this preliminary process, Knowhere aggregates stories from a continually repopulated and growing inventory of information and data points. News source websites are given a grade of trustworthiness. The aggregation can generate nearly a thousand stories with a spin of various political positions and persuasions to create a "knowledge graph" or database of each news story. A final editorial process checks spelling and grammar after the algorithm assembles the stories. Knowhere works by directing this AI system deployment to include amounts, rankings, statistics, and other figures. The output can be customized to fit a given bias, tone, or style.

Chapter 4

Addressing the Issue at the Intersection of Journalism and AI

I was keenly interested to learn whether and how thematic views are different among the publications, with a special focus on automated media generated by AI algorithmic system programming. My background in news and journalism started when I was in high school and evolved just after graduating from Columbia University School of Journalism (J-school) in the late nineties. I have worked for various media markets in the United States and have served as a correspondent for myriad international news networks. I observed that, through the years, nationally broadcast Black network news has struggled to be consistent. News and magazine publications have been steadily shrinking or disappearing.

These journalistic inconsistencies have created a void in mass communications, allowing predominantly white-owned and mainstream news companies to control the content of stories about the lives of Black Americans. This void of what I would refer to as Blackcentric (or Afrocentric) content created by Black-owned and Black-controlled news companies has generated questions about the placement of Black culture in media, especially how it is presented, received, and interpreted. Several companies such as BET, News One, Revolt, Black News Channel (BNC), and others have tried to mitigate anti-Black biases of omission in television news production by creating a national news and non-entertainment niche, but it has not endured the test of market rigors and financial benchmarks as discussed in the NPR story "The TV Network Black News Channel Goes Off the Air after 2 Years" (Chang, Levitt, & Fox, 2022). Print publications, such as *Ebony* and *Jet*, have filed for bankruptcy and are struggling to survive in their recognizable iconic forms. Exclusively Black newspapers are almost non-existent. Black online news content is underdeveloped.

American society has diverged from the common media practice of relying on newspapers, radio, and television for news and information content. Digital news has become an integral part of Americans' news media diets and social media platforms have played a vital role in news consumption. More people are receiving news from the internet on computers and smart devices. Social media sites have overtaken print newspapers as a news source for many Americans. Reports indicate that one in five US adults say that they get news via social media (Shearer & Grieco, 2019). The number of Americans using social media as their sole means of communication is slightly higher than those who do so from print newspapers. A 2017 study from the Pew Research Center showed that Black Americans were more likely than their white peers to follow up with action based on what they read in online news (Lu, 2017). The United States is becoming increasingly reliant on obtaining news from digital spaces and sources. With the mode of obtaining news and information changing in a fundamental way, Blackcentric news, especially that controlled by Black Americans, is threatened to be marginalized.

The evolution and increasing use of technology and news development has become apparent. This notion has been supported by academics who have explained that the use of algorithms in journalism is increasing with the trajectory of digital media access for information. Much of the content that algorithms use is published online. As technology develops and is implemented by corporations, much of the news on smartphones, tablets, and other digital devices will arrive via an algorithm to channel data and information. The Pew Research Center has indicated that more Black Americans are using digital and mobile technologies than their white peers. However, there is not much documentation regarding how this shift in news consumption is affecting this population.

As a member of the Black American community, I worked in newsrooms where coverage of the plights of the socioeconomically disadvantaged was ignored in favor of reporting on the interests of the corporate elite. For example, business stories were often preferred over stories that discussed the life challenges of the less advantaged. I rarely did stories about the homeless, but stories about crime and its connection to the Black community were discussed with frequency. What seemed to be missing were the stories of *success* coming from the Black community. In the variety of news content that comprises the US journalism industry, specific narratives from areas of the country that are facing disproportionate socioeconomic challenges are very often overlooked in favor of the interests of the elite and the advantaged. News and discussions about the stock market are given priority over conversations about how to improve the lives of the poor. These examples create a schema that guides smart computers in creating content. Without examination, humans may overlook the disproportionate coverage of some stories over others, but algorithms designed to collate news stories found from this asymmetry do not.

While researching the use of AI in journalism, this researcher observed that AI controversies extended as far back as the introduction of massive computer systems. Batya Friedman and philosopher Helen Nissenbaum (1996) reported concerns about computer systems being used for diverse tasks in the workplace, such as scheduling, employment matching, flight booking, and automated legal assistance for immigration purposes. Their criticism was targeted toward the procedures that these systems needed to generate results in the form of algorithms. They proposed a system of guidelines and procedures for addressing these issues. However, this researcher noted that cultural diversity was not part of the conversation in these guidelines.

As a professor who has taught at more than a half-dozen universities in the Washington, DC, metropolitan area and Pennsylvania, I have discussed the impact of media on pop culture, particularly how it manifests from the Black experience. One recent story that received a mountain of scrutiny was that of NBA hall-of-famer Kobe Bryant. After his death in 2020, the preferred way to discuss his legacy became a center of controversy. Discussions over how Bryant's life and death should be covered were in question. Should he have been considered only as a pioneering basketball player and loving father and husband or as a trail-blazing basketball player with a complicated background that included sexual assault allegations? Or should all of Bryant's highs and lows be presented equally without equivocation? Observations highlighting the importance of framing when discussing Bryant's legacy, especially as online content is accessible in perpetuity, need to be explored, especially when considering that algorithms cannot be programmed to adjust their final rendering of a story in accordance with context. "If robot journalism is not contextualized by human reporters with local knowledge, it easily leads to stories that get their facts right but fail to show the larger situation" (Fanta, 2018, 1). The imperativeness of providing more information to contextualize a person, an experience, or an issue becomes much more pertinent when considering the permanency of depiction. For now, humans are fully in control of what information is being provided and how. It is from this information that AI algorithmic processing is taking its cues. But with a background in journalism and communications studies, I realized the implications within communications when technology is given a larger role in journalism production. A question that scholars, industry professionals, journalists, and computer engineers alike are asking is, how will equitable representation look when human controls are diminished or eliminated and replaced by AI algorithmic processes?

I have also observed this issue through attending conferences such as NewsLab '20 and subscribing to numerous trade publications regarding AI and journalism. The study of algorithms in journalism is an emerging and growing area with indications that it will be studied much more aggressively in the future. Many newsrooms such as *The Washington Post, New York Times, ProPublica*, and others are experimenting with the technology to produce news reports or to assist journalists with their news coverage. However, issues about transparency and what data are being used to create news have not been widely discussed or studied. This is also happening alongside conversations dealing with diversity, equity, and inclusion (DEI) in our society. The DEI organizational framework was created to make spaces more inclusive of myriad members within our society. However, the concept of more inclusion while recognizing individuals' unique experiences has come under heavy scrutiny by lawmakers who support a white-dominated hegemonic socioeconomic caste system.

This research serves partly as an alert about emerging automated journalism methods that must be supervised responsibly to ensure that certain information and data are not ignored and restricted from the public. It also suggests that there needs to be even more vigilance than ever to safeguard the progress that our society has made throughout the years amid the indictment of a racial hierarchy. If the past is prologue, human biases will inevitably enter the complex and demanding needs of computer programming and algorithmic output. Concerns about the use of technology and its proper implementation have serious implications for communications, journalism, culture, and society.

Chapter 5

Artificial Intelligence in Journalism

AI is a type of technology that allows computer systems to perform tasks that usually require human intelligence to accomplish, such as speech recognition, decision making, and/or translation (Graefe, 2016; Norvig, 2012). This advanced type of computer programming makes it possible for computers and machines with onboard computers to learn from the tasks that they perform (Norvig, 2012). This type of learning allows the computer to calibrate itself to new inputs of information and to perform human-like tasks. Examples in the news include self-driving cars or computer-driven game competitions that use deep learning and natural language processing to help computers to understand, interpret, and manipulate human language. Using these technologies, computers can be trained to carry out customized tasks by processing vast quantities of data and recognizing patterns in the data sets (Graefe, 2016).

The process involved in automated journalism is dependent on a set of rules that are controlled to address a specific task. These rules are often created by engineers, journalists, editors, and computer programmers (Russell & Norvig, 2016). Computer programmers use linguistic samples and "translate them into a rule-based system that is capable of constructing sentences. If no such sample texts are available, trained journalists pre-write text modules and sample stories with the appropriate frames and language and adjust them to the official style guide of the publishing outlet" (Graefe, 2016).

Figure 5.1 shows how the basic functions of advanced natural language platforms such as NLP and natural language generation (NLG) operate through an algorithmic configuration in the final presentation of automated news content. The first step is data collection. "The starting point for NLG [natural language generation] is a database, for example sports, financial, weather, or traffic data. This data can be accessed via cloud or local memory.

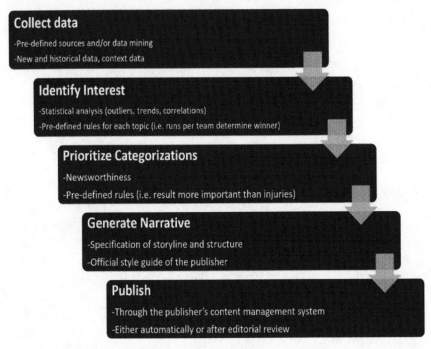

Figure 5.1   The News-Gathering Process of Automated Journalism

Then, it is processed according to predefined linguistic and statistical rules to a text in natural language" (Dörr, 2016).

Newsrooms have already used automated journalism techniques that incorporate NLG techniques, such as forecasting weather (Goldberg et al., 1994; Sripada et al., 2003). For a weather-related event such as an earthquake, certain data are collected for weather conditions in a certain region. In the second step, algorithms use statistical strategies to locate and highlight salient events within the data, such as the time of the earthquake, the size of the seismic shift, and climatic conditions. In the third step, software programming categorizes and gives priority to identified understandings by importance. Fourth, the prioritized topics are arranged to follow predefined rules to create a narrative. In the fifth step, the story or stories are uploaded to the publisher's content management system, which publishes the article (Graefe, 2016).

AI mimics human intelligence in assessing specific domains respective to its industry. It performs corresponding functions based on compatible programming. However, as an observation of changing media dynamics, some stories do not receive the same prominence as others, precluding specific and lesser-known narratives from being considered in the output of automated content.

In November 2016, the Chinese government held a workshop in Beijing focused on "Artificial Intelligence and the Future of the Media" with an experienced group of researchers, engineers, and experts from SAPPRFT (the State Administration of Press, Publication, Radio, Film and Television of the People's Republic of China), Renmin University of China, and the companies Microsoft, Baidu, Sina, EMC, and TRS (Zhou, 2017). The experts predicted that algorithms driven by a form of AI would play a major role in shaping the evolution of the media and journalism (Zhou, 2017).

Experts from the workshop discussed how advances in AI have orchestrated the way that algorithms can transform industries in which they are used (Zhou, 2017). Algorithms driven by AI have some fundamental advantages, such as increased speed of processing and information categorization to process large amounts of raw data efficiently in an autonomous manner, with no or little human intervention (Cohen & Feigenbaum, 2014). According to Cohen and Feigenbaum (2014), using a predetermined algorithm, AI can be used for simple journalistic tasks such as financial news and business reports. But there can be myriad uses where the functions of AI and algorithms intersect, and those uses are growing.

Kim and Cho (2000) cited myriad uses of AI to assist human engagement in media and journalism, such as repetitive tasks of looking for source information for an article. In that case, the use of AI diverges from conventional hardware-driven, robotic functionality. Instead of automating manual jobs, AI does frequent and rapid computerized tasks to replace manual labor. However, as Kim and Cho (2000) indicate, in this type of task performance it would still be necessary to manually set up the system and ask the AI program and its algorithmic functions the correct questions for it to carry out the desired objective. AI also adds "intelligence" or insight to certain functions. For example, a product using AI, such as the voice-activated device called Siri, made by Apple, enhances a music-listening experience. Through engagement of algorithms, AI refines searches for content (Graefe, 2016). In Carlson's (2015) descriptions of AI, adapting through progressively learning algorithms explains the programming.

AI finds patterns and consistencies in data so that the programmed algorithm can acquire a skill (Carlson, 2015). In this way, the algorithm becomes a classifier in some cases and an identifier in other cases (Carlson, 2015). Just as an algorithm can teach itself to play the historic Chinese board game "Go," algorithms can learn what news stories to recommend during a consumer's online perusal. These algorithmically based operations powered by AI can adapt when provided with new data. AI and algorithms specific to journalism have many hidden layers. Extensive data are required to develop deep learning models that instruct algorithmic functions (Carlson, 2015). The more data that are given to a request that is processed through the synergy of operations shared between AI and algorithms, the more accurate the output of the information will be.

While an increasing number of IT-based companies have accumulated large databases of customers and have become popular media platforms, traditional media have been facing a growing number of challenges as boundaries in the media and journalism industries have become justifiably more amorphous (Gray et al., 2017).

Several companies are using a form of AI and algorithm generation for user consumption (Graefe, 2016). The Associated Press is currently experimenting with and writing some stories with Automated Insights (Graefe, 2016). Automated Insights uses a program called Wordsmith that, according to Automated Insights' company managers, is "an artificial intelligence system that uses mounds of data, quantitative analysis, and some rules about style and good writing" to produce stories" (Ulanoff, 2014). AI companies such as Automated Insights, Narrative Science, or Yseop have already developed and deployed algorithms that create news stories in a matter of seconds while endeavoring to make the news gathering and news sharing process more efficient. It is important to note that even as the move towards enhanced efficiency may be steadily increasing, progress comes at a cost to accuracy and context when left unguided.

Monti (2019) reviewed the role of AI and algorithms in the *Washington Post*'s sports writing department using Heliograf, an automated news production system. Business executives are finding ways to use AI-driven software to push business interests in journalism. Covering sports is an attractive sector to supplement using algorithms because information can be easily broken down into numbers and statistics, creating new opportunities. Advancements that have been made in mathematics and statistical data have revealed new methods for analysts to make sharp and accurate predictions, which are also used by journalists.

Derived algorithms analyze copious amounts of data about a particular sport or event. These algorithms compile various factors, such as team and player statistics, injury announcements, weather experiences, etc. The sourcing for this data could come from numerous diverse sources. This includes official team and league websites, sports news platforms, and reporting outlets. Onwumechili wrote about this connection to sports and journalism, saying that "similar to the entertainment industry, sport is increasingly becoming commodified. Commodification means making something into a commodity and putting a price on it" (Onwumechili, 2017, 181).

Although Heliograf is not writing much of the *Washington Post*'s front-page content, the algorithmically based program is writing articles that are publishable. The use of AI and algorithms to manage automated journalism systems at the *Washington Post* has earned an award from The Big Data & AI

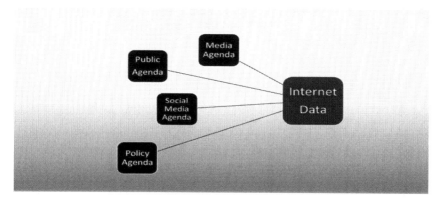

Figure 5.2 How Disseminated Public Sphere Information Is Collated into Internet Content

for Media Association (WashPostPR, 2018). The award recognizes the best practices in big data and AI products and strategies by media companies from around the world (WashPostPR, 2018).

According to scholars and industry experts, AI and algorithms work hand in hand in the production chain of automated journalism (Carlson, 2015; Graefe, 2016). Through software, news stories are created automatically by computers instead of human reporters. AI is programmed to search the internet for content and aggregate it (Carlson, 2015; Graefe, 2016). For this reason, the media agenda heavily influences what automated journalism produces. The example shown in figure 5.2 demonstrates the flow of quotidian media content to proliferate internet data. The daily media agenda shares similarities with the dominant information existing on the internet as sourcing material for computer programs to synthesize for news narratives.

This study does not focus on the various forms of AI or how social scientists debate the forms of this advanced form of computer functionality. This research focuses on the output of AI-developed news narratives. This is important because, presently, there is no existing scholarship on the thematic relationship between conventional news production methods and the automated journalism process, especially when evaluating the framing or impact on race and culture in journalism created by a means of production minimally influenced by human intervention. This study focuses on the output operations of algorithms that create news content, with the understanding that these algorithms are controlled, manipulated, and performed using a form of AI as explained by experts in the field (Carlson, 2015; Graefe, 2016).

Chapter 6

Media Representations of African Americans

Fair representation of Black Americans, which includes first, second, and third-generation Americans, who directly tie their identities to the lineage of enslaved Africans brought to America in the seventeenth century and Africans with a direct connection to the African continent, in media has often been a major issue within mainstream American culture and a major source of media bias. Biased media representation is often presented as a source of controversial material that disproportionately exacerbates negative portrayals of Black Americans in their communities. For example, in Thomas Hrach's (2016) book *The Riot Report and the News: How the Kerner Commission Changed Media Coverage of Black America*, he observed a singular incident during the 1965 Watts Riots:

> A television reporter encouraged two ten-year-old Black boys to stick their heads through a broken window because the picture would make interesting footage. Another cameraman asked the youngsters to take off their shirts and put on bandanas so they would look "bare-chested, piratical, and sinister." (12)

Hrach's (2016) breakdown is purposeful. Media have often been less than forgiving in their portrayals of Black people in America. At times, the presentation of African Americans has been insensitive (Pride & Wilson, 1997). As Smiley and Fakunle (2016) discussed, the synonymy of criminality with Black culture has a long-entrenched history in America. Historical documents record how hyperbole, stereotyping, and racism have led to discriminatory policies and court rulings that have fomented racial violence and created the growing increase of animus towards Black males, some of which still affects American society today (Wilson & Gutierrez, 1985). Myriad misconceptions and prejudices manufactured by the dominant class have been spread through various media conduits. Some depict Black men as brutes and thugs. Law enforcement agencies have disproportionately used deadly force on Black men who were considered to be "suspicious" or "of interest" (Smiley & Fakunle, 2016).

Despite research on the framing of Black Americans, there has been little research examining framing when it translates to automated narratives largely guided by algorithmic computation. If the editorial production of media trajectory stays on course, automated journalism will become commonplace. Despite the notions of a "post-racial" America, based on our history as a nation, it is important to recognize how emerging journalism would frame Black Americans without the benefit of human intervention in the editorial and story-crafting process. This research is a way to protect existing standards of social determinism over technology rather than its converse, technological determinism.

STATING CONTEMPORARY RELEVANCE

We are living in a digital era. The implications of how computer processing through AI and digitization are revolutionizing the media landscape are being realized, especially in the frame of news journalism media. As AI researcher Rajendra Akerkar (2018) stated, "The business adoption of AI is at a very early stage but growing at a significant rate. AI is steadily passing into everyday business use."

This research addresses diversity in information representation and access. Throughout history, members of subaltern cultures in the United States, particularly the Black American (or Black) community, have had to advocate for fair representation and access to information that is compatible with their needs as a community and society (Collective, B. S., 1995). Researchers and historians have long documented that Black citizens have struggled for parity in access to information.

Members of the Black press advocated on their behalf as early as the 1930s in order to cover salient issues related to federal agencies (Fields, 1944). They also had to fight for coverage of issues coming from their communities (Fields, 1944). But the struggle to produce and deliver Blackcentric content, Black-related content, or at the very least, information important to Black citizens, did not stop with print media. Radio continued a tradition of white dominance (Johnson, 1993) and television has followed in a similar fashion, including issues of ownership and access (McChesney, 2004). The expansion of the internet has inspired hope for true democratization of ethnocentric media interests, although intentions have not always met expectations. The impact, reach, and overall sense of equality are still being analyzed to validate those assertions and to improve the quality of digital information exchange. Some academicians remain dubious about the use of technology from the internet to deliver societal comity in mediated communications technologies (Skoric & Park, 2014).

Concerns about the presentation of Black or African American subject matter in news media and technological communications are not a new concern, but they are historically persisting ones. Race and hegemony have long been a part of discussions regarding the dearth of attention or the inaccuracy of information in communications media. Professor Molefi Asante (2011) wrote, "The Afrocentric idea positions intellectual discourse in the African agency that is often denied by Eurocentric conceptualizations of our roles" (22). Attempts to avoid emerging technologies in Western countries such as the United States are seemingly inevitable, as Langmia (2016) wrote, "Not to use and employ new communicative technologies is tantamount to the same accusation of primitivity that our forebears were tagged with in the 1930s" (62).

Lucy Dalglish, a professor and dean of the Philip Merrill College of Journalism, discussed the use of robots in newsrooms to improve efficiency and eliminate biases, an effort that she said has been in development for a decade (Seager, 2017). The term *robots* has been used to describe data-driven stories. But while the emphasis on discussions about automated journalism has centered on the speed, cost, and efficiency of data-driven journalism, dialogue about sociocultural impacts, as well as dialogue about cultural sensitivities and representation, has been nearly nonexistent.

Journalistic content created by automated journalism is mostly extant in large corporations that are run by financially and technologically elite members of society. As noted by Andreas Graefe (2016), large media corporations can manipulate the diversity of content that is produced for and distributed to the masses. It is important to understand the differences in content that is controlled and created by large companies utilizing advanced technologies and introduced to the masses versus content that comes from those without deep financial means and is offered using conventional methods (Akerkar, 2018).

Algorithms performing within the engine of artificial intelligence use data and assumptions to create content (Fritz & Foreword By-Brooks, 2002). This operation can lend itself to biases and inaccuracies in presented information, which could lead to journalistic outcomes that are undesirable and exclusionary to certain groups, even if unintentional (Fritz & Foreword By-Brooks, 2002).

In an automated piece in the *Romford Recorder,* for example, a story about students from socioeconomically challenged backgrounds attending a university included national statistics but did not connect other data, such as local disparities (Fanta, 2018). It also did not discuss other factors that have contributed to limits in students' access to colleges and universities, such as budgetary issues, which would have given the story contextualization. These informational disparities indicate a bias by omission about other statistical disparities. The author of the story, in critiquing the use of automated journalism, concluded that "robot reporting will never be entirely neutral, and its templates will reflect the political bias of its creators" (Fanta, 2018, 1).

So far, the mode in which algorithms perform tasks is based on a set of preprogrammed instructions and functions that prohibit specific queries within the technology itself to explain relationships or add contextualization about the presented information. However, the human mind processes things differently, the least of which is accomplished with more complexity. The aforementioned process is only part of what happens when audience members cogitatively frame their understanding of a story. Because algorithmic and AI technologies do not have the capacity to make decisions from enlightened decision making, they are limited in content creation capabilities operationally supported by NLG (Russell & Norvig, 2016).

This research is delimited to observing, examining, and comparing the manifestations of news narratives from companies with different means of technological production and sociocultural objectives regarding an experience of racial dynamism. Through deliberate examination of content from several news agencies during the week leading up to the US midterm elections of 2018, this study inspects the relevance of content created through automated means with news content that promotes its information to the public. This research was designed to understand not only how automated journalistic content presents news but also how it could potentially influence views about race through algorithm-driven narratives.

DEARTH OF AI IN JOURNALISM UNDERSTANDING

When Americans perceive a world of AI and algorithms, many concepts can come to mind: robotics, advanced computational equations, auto-piloted cars, and smart weaponry. The US government is earmarking billions of dollars to develop AI technologies and integration of them with existing technologies in myriad areas, including communications (Haner & Garcia, 2019). AI is predicted to be the defining technology of the twenty-first century in communications and automated journalism. This study looks at these mostly autonomously written narratives and how they compare to conventional publications.

Since the use of AI algorithms in journalism is a fairly new concept, concerns about its implementation have been discussed in industry, government, and academia. There are concerns about the cogency of automated content similar to conventional types of newsgathering. This research is concerned with understanding narratives created through the machinations of automated journalism, particularly the implications of this output regarding people and events that are intimately connected to American Black society. Automated journalism critics have expressed doubts as to whether AI algorithms used in journalism can be impartial, balanced, and free of errors that eventually influence the public sphere. These concerns have plagued the notion of written narratives for thousands of years ago, prompting Plato to question the legitimacy of the written word in the "Phaedrus" (Hackforth, 1972). Throughout human evolution, the written word has been studied, examined, and scrutinized. However, we are reaching an era in which humans may be the provenance of the material, but computer systems render the material for its final consumptive destination. Initial research has addressed issues of biases in automated journalism, but not in the way this research does by conducting a case study of a company that relies heavily on AI systems, algorithms, and their synergies to produce news narratives.

In a Nieman Reports article, the author pondered whether computers (or robots) would supplant journalists. This portent is one of the looming concerns among journalists and gatekeepers in the journalism industry, especially as data journalism has become a bigger part of the conversation when understanding the world around us through a media lens. It should be noted that smart machines, computers powered by AI to write content, cannot replace humans outright—at least not now, but this may not always be the case as technology develops. For now, machines still lack the ability to discern emotional or nuanced writing with perspective and contextualization. Research examining these writing styles and how they correspond to the American Black experience is limited.

Because of the journalism industry's drive to be technologically competitive in meeting the demands of information-hungry consumers, businesses will attempt to keep current with changing trends. Industry professionals will push to use the latest tools to stay up to date with their respective audiences. New communications technologies have often benefited the journalism industry. However, concerns over AI use may increase in the absence of research on the real effects of AI algorithms in journalism.

Algorithms replicate the styles of the programmers who write the programs the systems' technology is predicated upon. As an algorithm can write one version of a story, it can write several other versions based on its programming, as described later.

News narrative's editorial balance and programmed biases are among the initial concerns about the implementation of AI technology in journalism (Broussard, 2015). However, as technology advances, many improvements could and will be made in how AI algorithms in journalism operate. Some of the issues that are perceived with the introduction of "robot journalism" can be remedied with modifications guided by due diligence. There is a strong need for education in this area so that society is not making prejudiced decisions about automated journalism without understanding how it works, how it can be advantageous, how it can be shaped to benefit society, or how it can be potentially dangerous.

The purpose of this excursion into understanding differentiations between conventional online media sources and an automated journalistic source as they address the lives of Black American politicians and racialized events is to demonstrate the implications that are important in Black society and also our world. This study addresses a part of AI algorithmic expression in journalism by looking at a specific company and the framing of Black American political candidates and racialized events during the 2018 political election season. This addition to the epistemological branch of academic knowledge in this largely unexplored area at the intersection of artificial intelligence (AI), online news, and sociopolitical culture is but one step in understanding how computer systems managed by AI algorithms could play a role in the evolution of news journalism's narrative development, especially regarding Black American society and other marginalized populations. This study examined the following questions: (1) What themes emerged from racialized events that mentioned Black candidates during the 2018 US midterm elections? (2) Were the themes consistent among all three publication styles? (3) How did the Blackcentric, white-owned (mainstream), and automated publications use article/headline descriptors and article placement/length regarding Black candidates during the 2018 US midterm elections? (4) What are the differences in the frames between Black candidates in Blackcentric, white-owned, and automated publications during the 2018 US midterm elections?

Chapter 7

News Media and Race

When media are incorporated with hyper-capitalistic behaviors within a neoliberalist framework, the need for advertising revenues is apparent, as is the urgency to focus on the importance of media as a public good (Piketty, 2015). Within this process of money-making and techno-determinist dynamics, members or groups who do not have the technology or find themselves in a knowledge deficit will fall behind (Piketty, 2015). This research examines the use of artificial intelligence and algorithms in journalism when building news narratives that could preclude the unique experiences of Black people in the United States concomitant with deficient access to requisite technological knowledge.

Upon extensive review of books and literature, it revealed that there are very limited studies addressing the framing of race and Black candidates using algorithms in automated journalism platforms, especially when discussing US elections. Despite myriad studies on race and politics, the introduction of automated journalism has yet to be examined in detail. For example, Wingfield and Feagin (2012) looked at racial framing from a white (mainstream) perspective. They studied how Obama's election and assertions that the United States was in a post-racial society were not compatible with the realities of racism and anti-Blackness in the country. Other studies have looked at the framing of Black politicians such as Barack Obama (Ramasubramanian & Martinez, 2017).

Divergent perceptions of society in the context of racially diverse understandings of US culture demonstrate how some articles discussed problems associated with racism while others portrayed a "color-blind" society (Wingfield & Feagin, 2012). When the media introduce different narratives about a single topic, information may be interpreted differently. Bau et al. (2014) wrote that, "in addition to having a direct influence on democratic institutions

39

and practices, the impact of culture can also be indirect, that is, mediated by communication networks" (90). Despite the presence of research on automated journalism, no research analyzing or examining race in US culture through a prism of news journalism when using human intervention in production is diminished or eliminated was discovered.

McCombs et al. (2013) stated that, when the media introduce views or perspectives on a particular issue, they are shaping and determining what issues are important. Once this process is established, it continues to evaluate events. Computer programs are designed to use standards set by the media to generate news narratives, but there are no studies showing how this process could affect representation in journalistic output (McCombs et al., 2013).

The research incorporated in this book focuses on existing journalism publications and their framing of race. In two recent studies about the Black community, Holody et al. (2013) and Holt and Major (2010) reported acute disparities in how national media and local media covered events to frame the issue of race. Holody et al. (2013) discovered that newspapers framing race in their coverage of the 2007 Virginia Tech attack published more news stories about the shooting than did national newspapers. The local papers published articles for weeks after national newspapers had stopped reporting about the event. The national newspapers framed the race of the shooter, Seung-Hui Cho, more often and more prominently than did the local newspaper, even though it published fewer articles about the event. "The national newspapers also utilized the race frame more prominently, suggesting to their larger audiences that the race of the murderer was a significant factor in the shooting story" (Holody et al., 2013, 578).

Eargle et al. (2008) examined news coverage regarding the presidential candidates and how the news items varied according to the candidates' personal attributes. The data came from websites featuring four television news organizations (CBS News, CNN, FOX News, and MSNBC) for eight candidates (Obama, Clinton, Edwards, Richardson, McCain, Romney, Huckabee, and Giuliani). The testing period's duration was from August 2007 to September 2008. Eargle et al. (2008) found dissimilarities between the framing of "racial/ethnic minorities" and the treatment of individual characteristics.

Caliendo and McIlwain (2006) conducted a study that recognized differences in how President Barack Obama was framed in coverage about his bid in the 2008 presidential election. Newspaper coverage of biracial and all-Black elections were more likely to incorporate a racial frame than were stories about white candidates. The authors summarized their findings, indicating the close connections between "potential framing and priming effects" (Caliendo & McIlwain, 2006, p. 1).

Academics have recognized these reportorial nuances between racial demographics even at times when technologies' influence on the evolution of journalism was beginning to be realized (Latar, 2015). In the current condition, journalism that compares experiences of Black society to those of white communities is lacking when analyzing mainstream media narratives. There is historic and present evidence of this sociocultural neglect by the media (Latar, 2015). Presently, there is no nationally syndicated broadcast news programming focused solely on the Black community and the non-entertainment narratives stemming from it. American newspapers are struggling, as Donica Mensing wrote:

> In 1990 there were 1,611 daily newspapers in the United States with a circulation of 62.3 million; in 2011 that number had dropped by 229 papers and 18 million subscribers despite significant population growth. As a result, newsroom staffs have shrunk considerably: In 2000 there were 56,200 newspaper employees working for newspapers and by 2015 that number had dropped to 32,900. (as cited in Mensing, 2017, 220)

Black American newspapers, in keeping with usual American trends, are faring worse than their white counterparts (Wilson et al., 2012). The dearth of Black-oriented news could be obscured even more by the use of algorithms to develop journalistic content (Marshall, 2013).

Although Noble's research does not specifically explore algorithms in news journalism, her work examines data discrimination driven by algorithms that have the potential to become a serious social problem. Noble (2018) confronts the notion that search engines such as Google democratize access and the understanding of information. She contends that merging private interests in promoting specific types of information, along with restrictions programmed into algorithms, can result in a biased set of algorithmic expressions. She concludes that discrepancies in algorithmic functions discriminate against melanated people, specifically women of color.

Revelations regarding disparities in news coverage of race and members of the Black (African American) community were highlighted in the mid-twentieth century. The revelation was officially reported in 1967 by the National Advisory Commission on Civil Disorders Commission, also known as the Kerner Report. The first-of-its-kind report about the state of America cited factors that contributed to inequalities in society. One of the major disparities was in the mainstream media. "The press has too long basked in a White world looking out of it, if at all, with White men's eyes and White perspective" (NABJ Commemorates 50th Anniversary of the Kerner Commission Report, 2018). The advisory panel of one Black man and ten white men generated a report that stated that disparities in media should be responsibly addressed. It criticized media action that "the media report and write from the standpoint of a White man's world" (Report of the National Advisory Commission on Civil Disorders, 1968, p. 201–212).

Since that report, the climate has not changed greatly. Market dynamics concurrent with efforts to provide news to the Black community are doing a disservice to African Americans and Black Americans in what is considered to be a media political economy (McChesney, 2015). Comparatively, decreased production of news content and information with discourse from Black society falls short of America's idealism of full democracy and egalitarianism. Without efforts focused on inclusion, it is questionable whether the majority culture accepts the Black community, or other ethnicities, as fully accepted members of American society. "Exclusion from coverage in news media signifies exclusion from American society" (Wilson et al., 2003, p. 116).

This study was influenced by the emerging realities of technology's influence on the journalism industry. Noble (2018) wrote *Algorithms of Oppression: How Search Engines Reinforce Racism*. Her study, based on six years of research, looked at Google search algorithms. Noble argued that search algorithms can become racially discriminatory because they automatically reflect the biases and values of the people who create the algorithms. Noble (2018) pointed out that algorithms can reflect biases against women of color and people from other marginalized areas of society. Her research indicated that internet users could be influenced by racial and gender stereotypes, misrepresentation, and even economic redlining (Noble, 2018). Noble reported that Black Americans were discriminated against by algorithms more often than their white counterparts.

In 1965, a group of media researchers analyzed elements of international news stories to investigate what types of stories gained the most prominence. These stories were believed to set a worldwide "agenda." The researchers' findings helped them to develop a type of scoring system called *news values* (Lee & Choi, 2009). This news-based value system scores media content based on several factors that make content worthy of coverage by the media. A story that scored highly on each news value was more likely to make the front page or the start of a television news program.

News values are not the only factors that decide what stories earn distinction for news coverage. Journalists and news editors draw on their personal professional experiences to determine what should be considered most important or what should lead coverage saliency (Ardèvol-Abreu, 2015).

News organizations have their own news value system: (a) negativity: bad news receives more attention than good news; (b) proximity: stories that are relatively close to specific geographic coverage areas; (c) recency: newspapers are highly competitive about breaking novel news content; (d) currency: stories that remain in the attention of the public eye; (e) continuity: events that are likely to have a lasting impact on readers, such as a war; (f) uniqueness: a story that is unusual; (g) simplicity: stories that are easier to explain in bite-size pieces; (h) predictability: consumers expect to see certain news regarding an event; (i) elitism: stories about socioeconomically powerful countries or people; (j) exclusivity: being the sole outlet telling a specific story; and (k) size of story and the overall impact on the community or society. This news value system is shown in figure 7.1.

Despite this seemingly common system of what determines "news," what one newspaper displays on its front page may be different from what others display on theirs. In a digital age with the expansion of computers and real-time determinations, algorithmically based journalism is modifying the way that the prominence of news is determined by using data sets that access information from the internet.

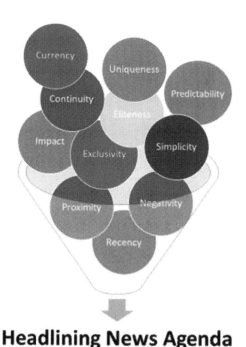

Headlining News Agenda

Figure 7.1   Understanding How News Values Determine the Media Agenda

Chapter 8

Agenda Setting and Framing

AI in Journalism

The method that Knowhere uses to take and reconstitute news from a variety of internet news media content makes agenda setting a compatible theory in studying the thematic output of its news narratives. Historical media academic scholar Walter Lippmann posited that the news media and the journalism industry were the main illustrators of the "pictures" in the public's minds (Lippmann, 2017). In Lippmann's seminal book *Public Opinion*, he discussed the rudiments of agenda setting, even though the concept was not as clearly stated then as it is today. Lippmann theorized that the news media acted as the public's window and thus included "framing" to understand a world outside of direct experience, and that this unique perspective helps a person to navigate the environment.

McCombs (1992) explained the news media creation of pseudo-environments where people may exist together in a certain space but think and feel differently about the space in which they co-exist. Scholars contend that this dynamic encourages thoughts that "respond not to the environment, but to the pseudo-environment constructed by the news media" (McCombs, 1992, 815). This theoretical framework is especially relevant to this study because of the way that media have become dominant in the public's perception of an agenda.

The agenda-setting concept can be analyzed on two levels: the agenda regarding objects or issues and the agenda of attributes. This research is interested in issues and the agenda of attributes that media content consumers place on the people or issues that they are reading about. These issues or the selected objects covered by the media could include, but do not exclude, coverage of publicly debated issues, individual political candidates, public institutions, or competing brands of goods (Ghanem, 1996). The research examining second-level agenda setting looks at the transfer of "attribute" salience from media to the public.

Researchers Kiousis (2004) and McCombs (1992) described attributes as "characteristics and traits that fill out the picture of each object." These attributes are also considered as a "set of perspectives or frames that journalists and the public employ to think about each object" (Ghanem, 1996, 17). Consequently, these attributes comprise specific characteristics from objects or issues. Agenda setting on the second level implies that unique attributes portrayed in media messaging are given more prominence than others. In essence, the attributes demonstrated in the media influence the public's understanding or perception of the issues. Subsequently, the first level of agenda setting, the agenda of objects, is connected to the transfer of salience of issues from the media to the public. Second-level agenda setting is concerned with specific attributes of an issue and how media coverage influences public thought regarding the issue.

Critics observing automated journalism's inchoate effects on journalism argue that the technology could be corrupted if it is not managed to remove biases and other anomalies that threaten accuracy or impartiality of content (Carlson, 2018). The distinct characteristics of Knowhere continually emphasize that the issues that it covers are connected to national and international interests corresponding to the public sphere. This is why the current coverage of Knowhere from the understanding of both levels within a theoretical framework is proficient as a case study. The first level of the study examines the framing of issues in the content covered through automated means and other conventional media means. The second level assists in explicating the various attributes associated with coverage in a thematic perspective.

This research also examines the relationship between Knowhere's coverage of issues related to the mainstream media and Black online news using metrics substantiated by agenda-setting theory. This provides an assessment of the basic concept of the agenda-setting theory, which connects the salient media agenda to public opinion. The analysis then extends agenda-setting studies into the second level or the agenda level where transference of attributes occurs. The study of an issue's attributes directs this study into the space of a framing premise.

This chapter includes an explanation of first-level agenda setting and a detailed explanation of the second level. These two explanations are important to understand the connections between the two levels and to reduce ambiguities about how the levels are related and eventually connected to framing.

FIRST-LEVEL AGENDA SETTING IN MASS MEDIA

Since McCombs and Shaw's (1972) seminal agenda-setting study, a compendium of research has been completed regarding agenda-setting theory. The legacy of agenda-setting work has been part of a tradition of many early social scientists who studied communications research, such as Lippmann (1922), Lazarsfeld and Merton (1948), Cohen (1963), McCombs and Shaw (1972), Cobb and Elder (1972), Funkhouser (1973), Noelle-Neumann (1973), and Rogers et al. (1993). This research continues the legacy of agenda-setting theory work and fills epistemological gaps as part of the growing research in the communications field. As the communications' domain continues to grow, the communications industry continues to modify, adapt, and grow with society and the technology that shapes it.

Agenda-setting deals with McComb and Shaw's (1972) basic premise that follows issues within the presence of mind transfer its level of salience from the media to the public sphere. The researchers posited that, if the media focused on selected issues in their news introductions, those same issues would be considered important by the audience. This approach in understanding agenda setting goes back to Lippmann's (1922) position that understandings of societal events are too sophisticated and confusing, so audiences need to rely on media interpretation and explanations to efficiently process the information that they receive. But it is important to point out that, when Lippmann made these proclamations about how people assess their environments through the lens of media, it was through the perspective of Western civilization and culture.

In the 1968 Chapel Hill Study, McCombs and Shaw (1972) interviewed more than one hundred residents in the Chapel Hill area twenty days before the presidential election. The researchers were curious to learn what the interviewees thought were the most relevant issues corresponding to their daily lives. McCombs and Shaw concluded in their highly regarded story that "the mass media set the agenda for each political campaign, influencing the salience of attitudes toward the political issues" (177).

McCombs and Shaw (1972) examined the content of four newspapers, two magazines, and two national broadcasts of evening news within the same time period. They cross-referenced two sets of data that included survey results and news content pertinent to the analyzed data set. Through a mathematical calculation, the researchers recognized that they had achieved an almost perfect consistency in the data, which led them to conclude that "the judgments of the voters seem to reflect the composite of the mass media coverage" (181). The pioneering social scientists' experiments and subsequent work changed the models of media research from the limited power of the mass media, which was popularly believed in early to mid-twentieth century, to the powerful position that the media can play in molding the public agenda (Lee, 2005).

There is evidence that people determine the relevance of issues from the salience or heightened presence that a topic receives. For example, the influence of the media depends not only on accessibility of data and information for a certain topic but also on agenda cues or agenda rationale (Pingree & Stoycheff, 2013). In the example of agenda cueing, data and information consumers approximate the importance of media issues based on the extent of coverage. Assumptions are made by observing how often an issue is mentioned (Gerbner & Gross, 1976; Pingree & Stoycheff, 2013). If the topic is observed and mentioned often, it is assumed to be important. This dynamic can be mitigated by distinct factors related to accessibility biases. This media effect can also be seen based on the medium in which the information is interpreted as having a level of importance (Pingree & Stoycheff, 2013).

Other agenda-setting research has had a place in civil rights issues. Winter and Eyal (1981) encouraged use of agenda setting beyond the limits that were set in the 1960s. They endeavored to find the best time span of agenda-setting effects, also known as lag time, when looking at issues about civil rights. Social scientists found that these issues ranged from 0 to 52 percent in the public's mind when comparing them to national public opinion in 1954 to 1976. When they compared stories on the front page of the *New York Times* with public opinion, they discovered that agenda-setting dynamics were prominent, especially within a four- to six-week period, which they described as "the optimal effect span or peak association between media and public emphasis of an issue" (377). The application of time duration to their study led studying researchers to conclude that "recent media emphasis rather than cumulative effects over time that leads to public salience" (381).

The leading effect of agenda-setting covers various types of media interactions on public issues that have been discussed in myriad studies since Winter and Eyal released their research. Eaton (1989) tracked the salience of eleven topics over a time frame of forty-two months during the 1980s. He found that the salience of ten of the eleven issues on the public agenda had positive connections with news coverage of the respective issues. In Germany, Brosius and Kepplinger (1995) evaluated killer and victim issues and found significant agenda setting for five main issues when the media agenda was matched to the concerns outlined in fifty-three weekly national polls.

Zucker (1978) took agenda-setting theory to another level by hypothesizing that agenda setting is limited to individual issues and events. He explained that the news media have a more robust agenda-setting effect for issues that are considered to be unobtrusive; that is, news to which individuals have limited or no personal exposure. Conversely, news that consists of obtrusive issues (issues that individuals experience directly) would restrain the effects of agenda setting in influencing the recipient. Consumers of media content tend to rely on the media for information on unobtrusive issues, but the way a person uses personal judgment and experience molds the framing of a story and shapes personal opinions about an "obtrusive" issue.

Other researchers followed in Zucker's footsteps. Yagade and Dozier (1990) renamed Zucker's defining terms from *obtrusive* and *unobtrusive* to *abstract* and *concrete*. They diverged from Zucker in their explanation of *abstract*. They explained it to be different from obtrusiveness, where abstractness is the level to which an issue is difficult to comprehend or process. They contended that concrete issues are concepts that people can easily understand and envision, such as the weather. Conversely, issues that are abstract are difficult in ways that people struggle to picture, such as intricate policy initiatives considered by Congress. When researchers examined daily elements of the news cycle, they discovered that concrete issues usually had a stronger agenda-setting degree of status than abstract issues. The study implies that the media may not actually set the agenda for issues that many would consider abstract. This nuance to the understanding of agenda setting is important because public issues that are important to people can also be considered as abstract or esoteric to the unaware. Connecting Knowhere to the concreteness of an issue could help to understand the news outlet's agenda-setting model.

Auh (1977) looked at things differently. This researcher from South Korea argued that conflict is a defining factor that augments the impact of agenda setting beyond mere coverage frequency. Researchers MacKuen and Coombs (1981) also found that stories that supported a level of conflict as part of the story had more influence on the audience than stories without a combative tone. That research suggests that stories that mainstream media cover in which there is an A versus B scenario would be picked up by Knowhere in a more facilitated fashion.

What is lacking in this area of mass communication research and where this research fills gaps is the examination of automated journalism and the framing of its stories collected from the mainstream media and influenced by the zeitgeist.

SECOND-LEVEL AGENDA SETTING IN MASS MEDIA

The agenda setting of objects and issues is relative to the attributes placed on them by the public. This process of attribute transference looks at the utility of studying frame changing throughout like events and among events that vary in their salience to the public (Kim et al., 2002). The agenda-setting dynamic can be envisioned as two concentric circles with Level 1 of agenda setting on the outside of the circle and Level 2 on the inside of the circle.

The outside shell can be explained as issues that are examined; the attributes ascribed to the issue are shown as happening inside of the shell.

In a similar characterization of the working dynamics within agenda setting, newspapers and television networks target large groups of audiences by gender, socioeconomic background, religion, and age. Media that appeals to this audience is called vertical media (McCombs et al., 1997) because they address audiences that engage in reading, watching, and listening. In contrast, horizontal media target special-interest audiences (McCombs et al., 1997). One example is news specifically about business, culinary interests, and even sports. It is evident that most media use both vertical and horizontal media to appeal to their audiences.

Research on second-level agenda setting concentrates on the transfer of "attribute" salience from media to the public (Kiousis, 2004). McCombs et al. (1997) described attributes as characteristics and qualities that complete the picture of an individual object. Attributes that are given by the public to media messages are the features or set of frames that journalists navigate to perceive notions about objects or issues (Ghanem, 1996). The basic premise of second-level agenda setting suggests that specific attributes that are depicted in media messaging are emphasized more than other issues. The attributes that are depicted in the media affect the public's perceptions of those issues. The second-level model suggests an extension of how the effects of agenda setting had been regarded previously. McCombs et al. (1997) modified Cohen's original assertions by restating agenda setting's overall impact: "The media not only tell us what to think about (first-level of agenda-setting-object/issue salience), they also tell us how to think about it (the second-level of agenda-setting-attribute salience)" (78).

The second level of agenda setting became evident when academicians investigated how attributes of an issue are transferred from the media to the public (McCombs et al., 1997). Second-level agenda setting can also deal with the way that it presents information, which is demonstrated in mass media. Ghanem and Evatt (1995) described this when they researched crime coverage in Texas. The study examined physical characteristics of the story, such as the location of the crime and other story details, to see the relationship between the crime perpetrator and crime victim. They found that determinants such as the aforementioned scenarios at the attribute level, the second level of agenda setting, were associated with the importance that the public connected to the issues of crime, considered to be at the first level. Ghanem (1996) discussed the dynamics between first- and second-level agenda setting in journalism news, similar to the depiction in figure 8.1.

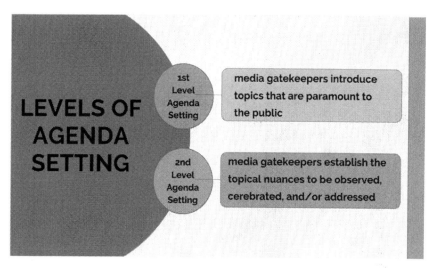

Figure 8.1   The Agenda-Setting Effect

Chapter 9

Agenda-Setting Theory and Framing Theory in Mass Media

In comparison to the larger body of contributions from academics, a minority of researchers have disputed the use of framing in research, taking the position that the framework is too limited in comparison to the factors that shape overall perceptions. However, Berkowitz (1984) contended that media presentation for the public to process, what de Vreese (2005) described as frame setting, holds the weight of content producers that frame stories and set the agenda just as much as the viewers attributing their perceptions to the content. Berkowitz's (1984) theoretical explanations were an attempt to develop a deeper level of understanding regarding framing to include the importance of the information's presentation instead of individual interpretation only.

The attributes of specific issues emphasized in the media share a similar contribution with frames exhibited in framing theory (Tankard et al., 1991). Tankard and his research associates were pioneering scholars who expanded on social scientist Ervin Goffman's 1974 framing concept. They described framing as "the central organizing idea for news content that supplies context and suggests what the issue is through the use of selection, emphasis, exclusion, and elaboration" (3). Knowhere claims that it reports similar news as other outlets with global operations with fewer human resources and less bias. However, critics of algorithmically based production say that the method by which news is collected, presented, and framed gives news a subjective quality (Miles, 2005).

Numerous scholars have demonstrated connections between second-level agenda setting and framing theory, as highlighted in this section. Framing theory looks at the choice and depiction of characteristics of issues and topics as is done in second-level agenda setting (Tuchman, 1978). Noelle-Neumann and Mathes (1987) discussed how media content can be examined at three distinct levels: agenda setting, focusing, and evaluation. Ghanem (1996)

53

studied how first-level agenda setting replaces the traditional view of agenda setting and how the subsequent two levels of agenda setting are considered under the direction of second-level agenda setting.

Myriad studies have inspected second-level agenda setting effects even before theorizing started in this computer-influenced domain. Successful research in this area has largely concentrated on presidential elections and the outlook of the US economy. With regard to presidential elections, Weaver et al. (1981) evaluated a nine-wave panel study looking at the agenda of attributes or characteristics of presidential candidates and the attributes that voters assigned to candidates. Several connections were found between the media agenda and the public's agenda, indicating that the direction of information flow traveled from the media agenda to the public agenda. Benton and Frazier (1976) examined topics centering on the economy and the attributes given to it. They inspected sub-issues connected to the economy, including problems, cause, and solutions. This closer look at sub-issues is likened to the focusing model discussed by Noelle-Neumann and Mathes (1987). Benton and Frazier (1976) also found connections between the media and the public agenda.

In a further exploration of how second-level agenda setting is connected to framing, Iyengar and Simon's (1993) research looked at various types of coverage of the Persian Gulf crisis. This was one of the first studies to implement second-level agenda setting as the theoretical framework for research involved in international affairs. Their study clarified and provided examples of differences between the primary and secondary levels of agenda setting. When audience members said that the Gulf crisis was the most important problem facing the United States, researchers described this as the first level. When audiences described the crisis in terms of military or diplomatic overtures, researchers described this as the second level.

Second-level agenda setting is not unidimensional. It is categorized by two main distinctions: substantive and affective (Ghanem, 1996). Substantive news is described as the characteristic of national publications that assists audiences to categorize news items and understand topics through graphics and pictures. Conversely, affective attributes are factors that elicit emotional responses from audience members. In the second level of agenda setting and literature examining political candidates' words, substantive areas are considered to be the candidates' ideology, qualifications, and personal characteristics, as explained by Ghanem (1996). He also explained how affective domains include tones (positive, negative, and neutral) in the way that candidates' representations are presented in news reports.

The nuances between substantive and affective domains are heavily influenced by audience members' need for orientation, which drives the reactive tendency for framing of certain issues and objects. The understanding that people need orientation demonstrates that they need to gain a sense of societal cohesion. McCombs et al. (1997) described this cohesion as a type of orientation that is dependent on two components: (a) how intimately a person connects to a specific issue, and (b) how much a person feels knowledgeable about the topic. Low relevance despite a feeling of uncertainty creates a low need for orientation; high relevance and low uncertainty provide only a moderate need for orientation; high relevance and high uncertainty result in an increased need for orientation. The researchers described how audience members who have an increased need for orientation about politics are more vulnerable to mass media agenda-setting influences than those with only a moderate desire for orientation. On the other side of the perspective, people with a moderate need for orientation are more sensitive to mass media agenda setting than are those with a low desire for orientation.

Lee (2005) examined relevance as personal involvement and uncertainty requiring knowledge. He introduced a third component: effort needed to cater to the messaging, referring to the accessibility of messaging to most of the public through various forms of media (newspapers, online media, television, radio, and other forms).

Numerous researchers, including the aforementioned Iyengar and Simon (1993), have distinctively documented and examined differences between first- and second-level agenda setting concepts by describing the attributes as "frames." These researchers and others clarified the concept that no comprehensive discussion about agenda setting is complete without interrogation of media frames and media framing. Ghanem (2002) posited that the differences between the research literature on frames and second-level agenda setting is that the second level evaluates the effects of news frames on the public agenda, and conventional agenda setting studies have concentrated on establishing the initial frames as they are presented.

FRAMING MECHANISMS IN JOURNALISM

The foundation of framing theory is that the media focuses awareness on particular events and then modifies the understanding of those events within a domain of meaning and comprehension. Framing is an essential topic in discussing agenda setting because it can have a strong influence on the public agenda, as well as on organizations and people. However, there are contrasting views and opinions on the effectiveness of framing. While some scholars contend that framing is too difficult to use, Dietram Scheufele (1999) argued that frames can have a substantive impact on what consumers and audience members believe when shaping a social reality. Scheufele (1999) wrote that there is an abundance of evidence derived from studies showing the impact of framing on an individual. He wrote that media frames help journalists to understand and categorize stories and ideas into comprehensive data. Scheufele and Tewksbury (2009), who took a theoretical position similar to that of Goffman, posited that individual frames are concepts stored in a person's mind to consume, process, and assimilate information. By examining media framing in this manner, it can be recognized as a perpetual cycle of presented information, the processing of that information, and the corresponding output that allows a reader to understand the world around them.

The second level of agenda setting to be considered when examining media frames justifies the emphasis given to issues in the media such as placement on the pages of newspapers or length of the story on a television newscast. The framing could even include repetition of a story that influences the prominence of the news item. The size of the article, how the sources are used, and the placement of a story in its respective domain could be factors in increasing the salience of the issue.

Another aspect of the relevance of a published article is the amount of attention that each source brings with views that support or criticize the narrative. This saliency of issues should be examined when studying social constructions deriving from the perception of issues within the media. Tankard et al. (1991) considered these focal points of news presentations and labeled them *framing mechanisms.* Agenda-setting research has focused on how often an issue is discussed in the media. The frequent mention of a topic has a more powerful effect than a framing mechanism (Gamson, 1989; Ghanem, 1996).

The framing concept is explained as part of agenda setting, but it augments the fundamentals of the research and the discoveries it yields. This analysis makes it easier to examine the possible consequences derived from the frames and who could benefit from certain framing to dominate the discourse. Frame analyses allow a media-engaged society to process how certain communication machinations mold worldviews.

The dynamics between agenda setting and framing could also be looked at in a context of inferences between the media that tell the public what to think about and, through framing, the media tell the public how to think about an issue. Academics who have studied agenda-setting in depth consider framing as the second level of the agenda-setting process. Patterson (1993) posited that "framing shares with agenda setting research a focus on public policy issues in the news and in the voters' minds. However, it expands beyond what people talk or think about by examining how they think and talk" (70).

Gamson and Modigliani (1989) examined what constituted a frame. They emphasized that every policy issue has an entrenched culture where the discourse progresses and modifies over a duration, discovering various interpretations or containers. "A package has an internal structure. At its core is a central organizing idea, or frame, for making sense of relevant events, suggesting what is at issue" (Gamson & Modigliani, 1989, 3). Tankard (2001) and McLeod (1987) also studied what comprised a frame. Hackett diverged from Gamson and Modigliani by saying that frames are closely connected to an individual's personal ideology, which he described as "a system of ideas, values, and propositions which is characteristic of a particular social class" (261). Essentially, Hackett contended that relevant news content is formed according to a common reality that the publics comprising society share, similar to an agreed-upon culture. An example of this would be a story angle or story line "which transforms an occurrence into a news event, and that, in turn, into a news report, is a frame" (Mendolsohn, 1993, 150). This is related, but in slight contrast, to Goffman's (1974) assertions that frames are more like strips in an individual's mind that organize information and define an event. The frames involved in various narratives are shaped by the editorial content that is directed by entities that control the information and how those gatekeepers decide to present it.

Looking further into framing theory suggests that the relevance of how an issue is introduced to the audience is called "the frame" (Goffman, 1974). This influences how people make decisions on how to process the information. Frames are an abstract concept that endeavors to categorize, organize, or structure the meaning of messages, including text and images. Frames are most commonly used in news or media when putting context to the information. Frames influence perceptions of news by the audience. Because of the way the information is processed, it is often considered as a second level of agenda setting. Whereas the first level tells one what to think about, the second level influences individuals on how they should think about the issue (Benton & Frazier, 1976).

Goffman first offered framing theory as a departure from traditional thinking about agenda setting while offering a concept that was connected to it. The framing procedural analysis helps to explain how people interpret what is happening in the world around them through their primary framework (Goffman, 1974). This type of framework is regarded as primary because it is taken for granted by the user; therefore, the framing paradigm does not depend on other frameworks to be functional in research analysis.

Goffman (1974) explained that there are two distinct separations within primary frameworks: natural and social. These two components encourage people to interpret information so that their unique experience can be comprehended in a broader social context, as suggested in figure 9.1, which expands the concept distributed in figure 8.1. What makes the two areas different are their functional roles (Goffman, 1974). For example, natural frameworks present events as physical occurrences that are interpreted literally and not given attribution. Social frameworks perceive events as issues that are driven by the public because of the demands, objectives, and manipulations by social

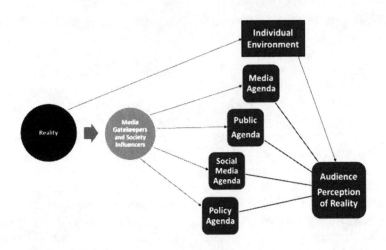

Figure 9.1   Setting the Agenda between Reality and Perceived Reality

players (Goffman, 1974). Goffman asserted that framing is responsible for society's interpretations of information. But Goffman warned that, despite this seemingly natural process, people who use framing do so casually, sometimes unconsciously.

Tiffen (1988) contended that the essence of news outturns is frames and angles. Cognitive psychology defines *frames* "as the function that specifies the relations that hold among arguments comprising a particular conceptual bundle at a particular level of abstraction" (Friedman, 1979, 321).

Entman (1993), a communication academician, suggested that "framing is the process of selection of a perceived reality in a way as to promote a particular definition, causal interpretation, moral evaluation, and/or treatment recommendation for the item described" (52). He explained how two categories of definitions have progressed: The first describes frames and how they affect audiences, while the second focuses on what constitutes the frame. Entman (1991) argued that "news slant significantly influences public opinion" (156). How events, issues, and people are framed influences people's minds as they process their environments. Studies have demonstrated that different phrasing of examined events leads people to make different choices (Machina, 1990). Situations that are introduced as "wins" influence people to think differently about the same situation than when presented in a frame of "losses" (Machina, 1990). This nuance regarding people's perceptions of problems produces predictable shifts of preferences, dependent on how a position is framed (Tversky et al., 1990). Tversky et al. posited that "risky prospects are characterized by their possible outcomes and by the probabilities of these outcomes" (72). The frames in news stories may also be nuanced and subtle, while still being powerful in shaping audience members' views (Pan & Kosicki, 1993).

News content consumers may understand bias in a specific narrative, but they may have difficulty in sensing the framing of a story. Similarly, social scientists have observed that word choice is important in questionnaires (Ghanem, 1996). Fine's (1992) research examined the impact of framing on public opinion regarding affirmative action programs. He concluded that the way questions and phrases are worded has a strong influence on how people perceive issues. In much the same way, the coverage of issues can apply to the production of news. The way that an issue is introduced or framed in the media influences how the public perceives the item (Iyengar & Simon, 1993). Entman (2007) expanded his research on framing to discuss the power dynamics involved in framing biases.

Wanta et al. (1993) studied the agenda-setting effect of international stories on Americans and discovered that similar types of story frames had a noticeable impact on the public through agenda setting. Patterson (1993) differentiated agenda setting and argued that every news story has a theme or frame that works as a central idea. However, the topic is typically the review label in the understanding of experiences regarding the story.

According to Fairhurst and Sarr (1996), framing can take many forms: metaphor, fictitious story, tradition (or ritual), slogan, artifact, contrast, or spin. The concept of framing is connected very closely to agenda setting theory (Scheufele & Tewksbury, 2009; Weaver, 2007). Both concentrate on how the media draw public attention to specific topics and set the agenda. Researchers have been studying how framing has become a communication tool for modern campaigns and how this changing dynamic has influenced agenda-setting relationships (McCombs, 2004; Price & Tewksbury, 1997; Scheufele, 2000).

One of the most prominently accepted definitions was introduced by Entman, who stated that frames "call attention to some aspects of reality while obscuring other elements, which might lead audiences to have different reactions" (Entman, 1993, p. 55).

How the media report on an issue has a mental effect on how the public reacts to received information. The current study raises questions of race coverage in an election cycle, looking at how the issue was reported and the corresponding attitudes that helped to shape the output and production of the narrative. The concepts of frames and attributes are often used interchangeably as academics study agenda setting. Entman's (1993) explanation linking agenda setting to news coverage could be illustrated in the following model.

Price and Tewksbury (1995) viewed agenda setting as a precursor to framing. Their assertions are common with those of numerous scholars who have studied the concept. Agenda setting examines story selection as a determinant of public perception. Framing highlights which topics or issues are picked for coverage by the news media. Instead of only the specific ways that issues are presented, it is necessary to factor in how public issues are crafted for the media audience (Wanta et al., 1993). This would mean that story frames are conditional in event or issue presentation to understand the agenda-setting concept. Frames are a necessary part of the interconnected agenda-setting process, not an independent entity.

Framing takes the agenda setting concept a step farther in how news texts can be presented when creating a frame for information. This is because the power of the media can influence various public interpretations of a specific event depending on the frame it is presented within. This can be a conscious decision by people who deliver news, such as reporters. In this way, a frame corresponds to the way that gatekeepers categorize and present ideas, events, and topics. For this reason, framing is the method by which communications sources define and then assemble a piece of information to be interpreted. This process is imminent when being introduced to new information; it is a process that all humans do. The manner in which a problem is framed could direct how people understand and evaluate the problem.

Agenda setting's first level deals with the selection of issues and the impact on the public agenda. Agenda setting's second level deals with the selection of attributions for elements on an individual issue or set of issues. In the current study, I employ the word "frame" synonymously with the word "attribute." Hendrickson (1995) stated, "Characterizing all media content, or even one story on a particular topic or issue with any frame overlooks a great deal of complexity and subtlety" (3). This is why it is important to analyze headlines and corresponding articles from several angles. Bateson (1972) explained the concept of framing as a "cognitive window" through which news is "seen" (59). A frame could also be viewed according to how other theorists and social scientists have explained it: as a picture frame that incorporates some elements of reality while precluding other elements (Gamson, 1985; Gerhards & Rucht, 1992; Patterson, 1993).

A picture frame influences the perceptions of what is included within the frame and affects how the full picture is viewed. For example, an elaborate picture frame can make a picture look different from how it would look in a simple frame. Similarly, the amount of attention paid to a story, how it is positioned in the publication, its texture, how it is angled, or patterns in the frame influence how a story is pictured, perceived, or framed (Ghanem, 1996).

According to Ghanem (1996), media frames can be deconstructed into the topic of a specific news item, framing constructs, and framing attributes, including size and placement, substantive attributes, and affective attributes. Ghanem's paradigm explains the agenda setting concept by itself, as well as the understanding of first- and second-level agenda setting. I categorized various major elements of framing that can be considered attribution levels of primary agenda setting or second-level agenda setting.

One of the drawbacks in framing studies is that attribution of an issue cannot be generalized. Although subdimensions cannot be generalized, the four areas of framing or of attributes—subtopics, framing mechanisms, affective dimension, and substantive dimension—could underlie comprehension of aspects of specific frames in news media.

THEMATIC AND EPISODIC FRAMING

In addition to myriad frames that can be created by the individual crafting a desired narrative, numerous frames can play a part in how a story is written and interpreted. Using thematic and episodic framing can influence how an audience member responds to a story. Thematic framing concentrates on events and issues in a broader contextualization. For example, a thematic frame could be discussed in terms of racial disparities rather than just as a person's racial identity. Episodic framing is a bit different. Episodic framing focuses on a particular example of a specific issue. Shanto Iyengar (1991), an American political scientist, wrote that episodic framing takes on the form of a situation or event-oriented report and portrays public issues as concrete issues, such as the experience of a single mother living in poverty, an opioid addict, a mass shooting, or a plane crash. Conversely, a thematic frame puts public issues in a more general or abstract space. These thematic news frames "place public issues in some more general or abstract context and take the form of a 'takeout,' or 'backgrounder,' report directed at general outcomes or conditions" (Iyengar, 1991, 14). These thematic paradigms include reports on changes in government policy on affirmative action, reducing mass incarceration, or workplace racism but could also include domestic policy issues in Congress or sociopolitical concerns about immigration. A key difference between episodic and thematic framing is that episodic framing portrays events that showcase issues while thematic framing presents collective or general awareness. Iyengar differentiated episodic and thematic news framing as a comparison in which "visually, episodic reports make good pictures, while thematic reports feature talking heads" (Iyengar, 1991, 14). It is important to emphasize that many stories contain both elements of thematic and episodic framing, although in most cases, one frame is more dominant than the other.

Iyengar (1994) contended that it is rare for a news report to be only thematic or episodic. For example, in the case of a single mother living in poverty, the story could be framed with problems of poverty across the

United States. Another story with the same woman as the center of the narrative could address problems of budgetary funding cuts in local and federal government. In most cases, one frame clearly predominates (Iyengar, 1991). Scholars note that episodic framing influences less willingness to hold public officials responsible for ameliorating social problems or blaming them for persisting undesirable issues (Iyengar, 1991).

In an experiment examining the effects of episodic and thematic framing, Iyengar (1991) discovered that episodic framing spotlighted a need for audience members to emphasize individual responsibility for news narratives about white American criminals and due process within the US legal system. Conversely, he found that episodic framing regarding Black criminality and illicit drug use was limited. Iyengar attributed this difference to the observation that audiences were already more likely to hold individuals responsible in situations of illegal drug use and crime committed by African Americans. However, Iyengar also noted that consumers of an episodic frame of the story were less likely to discuss societal reasons for crime in their description of the event.

Lene Aaroe (2011), an academician who studied thematic analysis extensively, found that episodic frames that successfully established an emotional response in the audience were the most effective at influencing opinions. However, when there was not a strong emotional attachment to the frame, thematic framing was more influential in how an individual perceived a particular story.

Researchers Paul Brewer and Kimberly Gross (2005) conducted an experiment to evaluate whether episodic frames developed a different emotional impact than those created with thematic frames. She gave respondents three articles about mandatory minimum sentences. The first was an episodic story about Janet Smith, a white woman who faced a mandatory fourteen-year sentence for being an accomplice to her boyfriend who dealt drugs. The second article offered the same dynamics as in the first story except that Janet Smith was depicted as a Black woman. The third article offered the same story using a thematic frame. Gross found that there were greater emotional responses to the episodic stories, and there was little difference in the emotional responses to stories about Janet Smith regardless of the racial differences in the way that Smith was portrayed.

In 2008, Gross conducted a similar experiment but added a test to evaluate the emotional reactions of readers. This experiment demonstrated that episodic framing was more emotionally connected and influential in shaping opinions in an opinion-based news story format. In Gross's experiments, the thematic and episodic pieces were formed to influence opinions against mandatory sentencing. In weighing emotional responses by participants, thematic frames were more persuasive than episodic frames (Gross, 2008). Gross found that race was viewed differently in thematic and episodic framing depending on whether the pieces were fact based or opinion based. Gross's framework explained thematic relationships deriving from framing as examined in this study focused on race. The upcoming chapters examine how different online platforms contemporaneously framed the intersection of race and politics.

Chapter 10

Blackcentric Media

AFRO.COM

Articles featuring Black politicians were placed high up on the webpages of Afromedia/Blackcentric sources. The two weeks leading up to election day in 2018 provided many stories that led the headlines of this publication, such as "NBC Cancels Megyn Kelly's Show After Blackface Controversy" (Elber & Kennedy, 2018). A departure from the mix of hard news, sports, and entertainment prevailed during this time period. Featured articles that included Black candidates were about seven hundred words in length. The descriptors of Black candidates were obvious and easy to identify. Headlines such as "Kamala Harris in South Carolina" or "Ben Jealous for Governor" (2018) from *The Afro* using the domain: Afro.com occupied the front page and were featured prominently above other headlining news items. This pattern was consistent with articles that featured former President Barack Obama and former Florida gubernatorial candidate Andrew Gillum. The articles from Afro .com tended to be six to eight hundred words in length. Most often, Black candidates were portrayed as leaders with guiding principles that would save America from itself, such as the article that highlighted Harris's run for President. In the Afro.com article "Kamala Harris in South Carolina: 'Fight for . . . who we are'" Harris's candidacy was the focus (Barrow & Kinnard, 2018). Although the story did not discuss the details of a Harris run for president, an effort that would be fulfilled in the beginning of 2019, Harris was discussed as a potential candidate who would help to restore the soul to the core of America. "This is a moment that is really requiring us as a country, as individuals, to look in the mirror and to collectively answer a question: Who are we?" (Barrow & Kinnard, 2018).

Articles from *The Afro* featuring former gubernatorial candidate Stacey Abrams were always found in the list of top stories on the front page. However, although Abrams was mentioned in several articles, she was seldom depicted as the protagonist of the narrative. She was often discussed as the victim of voter schemes. Some of Abrams' descriptive words from Blackcentric (Afrocentric) media are shown in the word cloud in figure 10.1. In the story "Georgia Election Fight Shows That Black Voter Suppression Still Flourishes," introduced as a special report, Abrams's presence in the story was not as the main character. The story sat prominently high on the front page but did not discuss in specific detail about the Abrams candidacy. The only line in the story that mentioned Abrams was: "Kemp, who is running for governor against Democrat Stacey Abrams, says his actions comply with a 2017 state law that requires voter registration information to match exactly with data from the Department of Motor Vehicles or Social Security Administration" (Knight, 2018).

The other Afro.com article that featured Abrams was placed high on the page. This article combined celebrity and politics. In "Voters Raise Concerns About Voting Machines, Poll Access," the word count was 900, a bit longer than the usual seven-hundred-word count. Abrams' role was understated in this article, which focused on voter suppression. Although Abrams was talked about in this article and would have been adversely affected by deficits in voting, there was little mention of who Abrams was as a candidate or a person. This diminution of Abrams' personal qualities in the article indicates that Afro.com's attention was less on the candidate's unique behaviorisms and more on voting conditions. Even in the article "Obama Urges Georgia Voters to Elect 1st Black Female Governor," Abrams is seen as the recipient of secondary focus after the former US President Barack Obama. In this narrative, the headline that featured Obama and not Abrams was near the top of the page, surpassing headlines dealing with entertainment, sports, and other stories of interest.

Afro.com also used articles and headlines more descriptively when highlighting Ben Jealous, whose publications followed him steadily during the studied time period. In the article "Jealous Running Hard in the Final Days of the Campaign, Even as Polls Point to Hogan," the Jealous headline is featured prominently on the front page close to the top of the cover page. This article was 723 words long.

Another Afro.com article, "Black Women Save Politics," focused on the determination of African American women to change the political climate. This article was 743 words in length. It depicted the women as brave and intrepid defenders of the democratic process, using words such as "strongest" and "powerful" (Green, 2018). Afro.com's highlighting of Black candidates indicated that the publication was unabashed in its coverage and not hesitant to address issues such as racial inequality.

Figure 10.1 Black Media Describes US Presidential Candidate Stacey Abrams in a Word Cloud

An assessment of article and headline descriptors for Ben Jealous yielded similar results. As the campaigning season became more intense, the number of headlines and their proximity to the top of the front pages became more apparent. Headlines such as "Ben Jealous for Governor" and "Jealous

Running Hard in Final Days of the Campaign, Even as Polls Point to Hogan" revealed the stance of the publication. These headlines were placed above entertainment items about big-name celebrities. The narratives often discussed Jealous' background and his staunch advocacy for the disenfranchised. Afro.com's conspicuous coverage of Ben Jealous was apparent as it discussed Jealous's determination despite him being behind in the polls. The use of the headline here showcased the publication's support for the candidate.

THEGRIO.COM

TheGrio.com used descriptive headlines with more frequency than did Afro.com. "Can Stacey Abrams Win Over White Voters in the South? This Supporter Says 'Yes'" was a headline on October 31, 2018. This article, at 348 words, was shorter than the Afro.com articles, but it also featured a video. This headline depicted Abrams as more of a champion or a successful politician than did the portrayals in Afro.com. Other articles discussing Abrams in TheGrio.com gave her more visibility when it related to Black candidates.

TheGrio.com openly highlighted Black candidates who fought to take on the establishment candidate, who was often conservative, white, and Republican. In "Too Close to Call? Stacey Abrams Leads Brian Kemp by Just 1 Point in Georgia Governor's Race," the publication stated its preference for Abrams over Kemp, predicting improvement in policies for Black Americans in Georgia if she were to be elected (Telusma, 2018). The narrative implied that the race was too close to call. It highlighted Abrams' endorsements rather than those for rival Kemp. These articles were longer than other articles that were less politically influenced. However, the stories were generally positive in their representations, rather than neutral or negative in tone.

THEROOT.COM

TheRoot.com featured headlines and articles discussing racial issues during the campaign season. Many of the articles featuring Andrew Gillum and Stacey Abrams, for example, were placed close to the top of the page, indicating priority over other stories. The headlines always featured the candidates' names and their relationships to the racial issues contemporaneously discussed in the media. An example of the prominence of candidates and race on the front page and cover page of TheRoot.com was "The Governor's Debate Between Stacey Abrams and Brian Kemp Is Everything That's Wrong with Georgia Politics" (Johnson, 2018). When this story appeared on October 28,

2018, it was listed as one of the top five stories on the cover page, showing a level of importance assigned by the editors and publishers. Black candidates were depicted in mostly positive references.

The Root gave other stories surrounding race and the election a level of attention. Other stories such as *"Today* Addresses Megyn Kellys Blackface Comments; Kelly Tearfully Apologizes," and "Brian Kemp Launches Investigation into Georgia's Democratic Party for Vote-Hacking and Everyone Knows Why" sustained the theme of voter suppression through election day while addressing ignorance and outrage surrounding racialized events in American society. These were significant topics within the context of a competitive political election.

The importance of choosing preferential stories over the content of other narratives was associated with the type of media from which they were aggregated. The issue of blackface and its pernicious foundations was more prominent in TheRoot.com, indicated by the red arrow, than in USAToday.c om or Knowhere's coverage on October 25, 2018. The controversy surrounding Megyn Kelly and her query about the appropriateness of blackface was high up on the front and cover page of TheRoot.com. This story was given prominence over others.

This suggests that the topic of blackface was important to the publishers. In the USAToday.com article regarding blackface on the same day indicated by the red arrow, the story is lower on the page and not given the same level of prominence as in TheRoot.com. Immigration rights, celebrity relationships, and international news were all presented in headlines above the blackface issue. Addressing blackface was not even on the list of USAToday's "Top Stories." This indicates that, in the minds of the media gatekeepers of this publication, the issue of blackface was not as important as it was in the Blackcentric publication, TheRoot.com. For Knowhere, the blackface issue was not a leading story on the website's cover page. This supports inferences about the stated functioning of Knowhere's AI algorithm to take its referential news coverage from mainstream reportage.

Chapter 11

White-Owned Mainstream Media

Coverage from white-owned mainstream media was often longer than that in Black-owned media. For instance, articles from the *New York Times* were the longest of the white-owned publications, averaging more than one thousand words. NewYorkTimes.com is considered one of the pre-eminent publications in the United States, eighteenth in the world and third in the country, with a circulation of 487,000 (Watson, 2019). It is often described as left-leaning, but it is considered a newspaper of record because of its wide circulation, its in-depth coverage of political events, and a long-established record of reporting. Issues involving race are often placed high on the cover page of the website. During the research time duration, headlines often featured Stacey Abrams more than Andrew Gillum or Ben Jealous and were neutral in their expression. For example, in the *New York Times* article "Stacey Abrams and Brian Kemp Renew Attacks in Georgia Debate," the article discusses the candidates with equal attention.

Black candidates were largely covered similarly to non-Black candidates. For example, in the first week of the material that this study covers, there was a headline every day that reflected either a candidate or an issue that was directly connected to the Black experience in America.

In the *New York Times* story, "Abrams, a Daughter of the South, Asks Georgia to Change," the headline is featured prominently at the top of the page in the leading section of the cover page and features more than three thousand words (Sarah Lyall & Fausset, 2018). Gillum's coverage in the *New York Times* was sometimes less neutral. The headline "Messages Raise New Questions Over Andrew Gillum's Lobbyist Connections" depicted an embattled gubernatorial candidate who was under investigation by the FBI. Other headlines about Gillum, such as "Andrew Gillum's 'Hamilton' Ticket Came From FBI Undercover Agent, Text Message Shows" and "Andrew Gillum and Ron DeSantis Trade Attacks Over Corruption and Racism in Florida Debate" indicate that the descriptors of Gillum were not always neutral in discussing his actions on the campaign trail.

USATODAY.COM

USAToday.com is largely headline deficient in emphasizing the presence or prominence of Black American candidates. In the only headline during the study's time period, "Racist Robocall Targets Stacey Abrams, Oprah," the nationally distributed publication featured this story regarding Abrams' alliance with Oprah Winfrey and how they were the victims of racist verbal attacks by telephone (Cummings, 2018). This article was about 600 words in length. The lack of other headlines pertaining to Black candidates during this time period indicates the level of importance assigned to them by the publishers.

WASHINGTONTIMES.COM

This white-owned/mainstream publication, which is considered right-leaning, increased its coverage of political news during the studied timeframe. Narratives during that time period often put Black candidates on the front page, regardless of their respective political affiliations. However, Democratic candidates received the most attention, allowing for more readership attention over lesser-covered candidates, such as conservative Utah politician Mia Love.

Headlines featuring Black candidates appeared on the front pages of the *Washington Times*. However, these headlines were less prominent than those that featured the president or other political issues. For example, in the two weeks that were studied, it was rare to see a Black political candidate given a level of heightened prominence, and that was revealed for both Democrat and Republican candidates. On November 6, 2018, a GOP candidate made it to the cover page of the *Washington Times* but lower on the page from the prominent headlines. This area of the *Washington Times* cover page often featured the agenda of the President of the United States. The article "Michigan Paper Fires Reporter for Bias Against GOP Senate Candidate John James" presented a discussion about an apparent bias issue. This article regards one of the reporters who had made insulting comments about James when she wrongly recounted a conversation during a telephone conversation that had ended (Varney, 2018). The article's length was less than 124 words. Despite the inclusion of a Black GOP candidate, this was the only mention of this candidate during the time period, demonstrating limited attention regarding this candidate and other Black candidates running concurrently throughout the country.

The article featuring James was neutral in tone. However, other articles featuring candidates such as Stacey Abrams and Senator Kamala Harris were negative. These articles were placed on the front pages and in some cases featured quite prominently. One of the leading articles in the *Washington Times* during this period, featured in the "Most Popular" section on the cover page of the publication on October 23, 2018, was "Stacy Abrams Admits She Burned Georgia State Flag in College" (Morton, 2018). This article was 321 words in length. Another article featured on the front page on the same day was entitled "Andrew Gillum's 'Hamilton' Ticket Came from FBI Under-cover Agent, Text Message Shows" (Brown, 2018). This negative depiction of Gillum, in 220 words, followed the controversy of his receipt of a coveted ticket for a popular Broadway musical. A little lower on the cover page, a second article featured Gillum in an article titled, "Andrew Gillum Still Holds Lead in Florida's Gubernatorial Race, Poll Shows" (Varney, 2018). This article was 263 words in length. Although the article was neutral in tone, it was placed lower than other articles with more negative tones regarding both Gillum and Abrams. On the same day, sharing the cover page, a lesser-known candidate was discussed in the article "Monique Johns, Dem Candidate, Caught Taking Republican State Rep's Campaign Material" (Ernst, 2018). This article contained 214 words. Although it was shorter than most written articles in the *Washington Times*, John's actions were covered on the front page and in the "Most Popular" section of the online publication. This suggests that the depictions of the Black candidates were more negative in terms of their coverage than neutral or positive.

Chapter 12

Automated Expressions in Journalism

Headlines were fairly neutral in the automated news content in Knowher-enews.com. For example, the story that discussed Stacey Abrams's flag burning past was headlined: "Stacey Abrams, Brian Kemp to Meet in TV Debate" (Knowhere, 2018). This story was about 250 words long and focused heavily on the contentious race between Abrams and her rival for the Georgia governorship, Brian Kemp. In the other story offered during the time period of this research regarding Stacey Abrams, the headline was, "Pence, Oprah Campaign in Georgia Governor Race" (Knowhere, 2018). This article was basically a brief; just less than 250 words in length and focused more on Oprah Winfrey than on Abrams. The largest paragraph in the story reads:

> Meanwhile, Winfrey, campaigning for Abrams in Marietta, received lots of coverage from cable news channels and gave a speech explaining her support for Abrams, who is seeking to become the first black woman to be elected governor. "I am here today because of Stacey Abrams," Winfrey said. "I am here today because of the men and because of the women who were lynched, who were humiliated, who were discriminated against, who were suppressed, who were repressed and oppressed for the right for the equality at the polls." (Knowhere, 2018)

Although this story contains quotes from Oprah Winfrey, Brian Kemp, and Kemp's campaign advocate, Vice President Mike Pence, at the time, it contained no quotation from Abrams and focused on Winfrey's campaigning on her behalf. This omission of Abrams was similar to the social constructions in mainstream narratives about Abrams.

Knowherenews.com often has three headlines for each story. At times, it offers only one—a convergence of its left- and right-leaning narratives into a neutral narrative. Because the news article count was less than that for the conventional counterparts, every headline studied for this research was featured prominently on the automated publication's cover page.

The coverage of Andrew Gillum by KnowhereNews.com was similar to the coverage of Abrams in the other publications. In the article "Trump Calls Florida Gubernatorial Candidate Andrew Gillum a 'Thief,'" the narrative focuses on Trump's unsubstantiated claim that Gillum is corrupt, but it does not report Gillum's stance or rebuttal to the accusation. The article, less than 200 words in length, detailed the president's post about Gillum, a quotation from the president, the education level of Gillum's opponent, and a mention of Gillum's race.

Trump posted:

> In Florida there is a choice between a Harvard/Yale educated man named @ RonDeSantisFL, who has been a great Congressman, and will be a great Governor and a Dem who is a thief and who is Mayor of poorly run Tallahassee, said to be one of the most corrupt cities in the Country! (Knowhere, 2018)

This is one of the few articles that Knowhere provided regarding Gillam's ambitions and attitudes towards adversarial Republican discourse during the researched time frame. Although it reported that Gillum had a slight edge over his rival, the headline and article focused more on Gillum's competition than on his campaign promises and objectives.

Headlines for Black candidates' articles tended to appear on the cover pages of the automated news content. Most headlines were neutral. However, some Black candidates were mentioned in negative headlines. Knowhere's headlines are not as numerous as those in the conventional media. Whereas there would be dozens of headlines on a NewYorkTimes.com cover page, there are fewer than ten headlines on a Knowhere article covering nationwide news.

BLACKCENTRIC AUTOMATED MEDIA FRAMING

The framing of Stacey Abrams in Blackcentric media was that of a "great uniter." In contrast to the derisive term "social justice warrior," the frame of "the great uniter" has a more positive connotation. For example, in the article from TheRoot.com,

> There are more than 400 black women running for public office, but none of them reflects the essence of their collective campaigns more than Abrams. At 44 years old, she stands to be the first black woman to lead a state in America's history if she wins. That's an astonishing possibility to the many people here who remember Lester Maddox, the segregationist governor who resisted integration

so fiercely, he once ran black people out of his restaurants with a pistol. (Starr, 2018)

Articles that focused on Abrams's position in the Georgia gubernatorial race often discussed her desire for progressive values focused on inclusivity. These articles discussed alleged voter suppression efforts on behalf of her political rival and Election Commission administrator Brian Kemp. Stephen Crockett Jr.'s article was in concert with other articles that put Abrams in a social justice champion frame. The story's discussion of Abrams addressed the dynamics of hegemony and oppression, a characterization often associated with the Deep South (Henry Wallace Taking Crusade into Deep South, 1947, 18).

In another article from TheRoot.com, reporter Jason Johnson described Abrams as a unifying candidate who advocates for people living in lower socioeconomic brackets.

On the merits, Stacey Abrams won. She effectively answered questions about her finances, the history of her voter registration organizations and laid out a few plans for criminal justice reform and tackling drug addiction in Georgia. (Johnson, 2018)

The framing provided by Black American media indicated that Abrams had a responsibility to challenge usual stereotypes such as the "welfare queen" trope that was popularized during the Reagan administration after a speech the former president gave. Black women in American politics often exhibit the ability to diminish their own marginalization to become more attractive to voters. By connecting equanimity and oppression, Black American media have associated Abrams within the frame of an individual who could defeat their oppressive experience and embrace their desired status.

Black American media framed Abrams as one who deserved to be treated as an equal but who could also fight for others who endeavor to counter narratives of victimization and oppression. The frame tends to favor a person whose personality unites those who are looking to challenge oppression through socioeconomic and sociopolitical separation. Despite pressure and stress arising from the expectation to prove themselves as equal members of society, Abrams is framed as a woman candidate with the ability to break barriers and bring together the rights and experiences of diverse peoples.

When examining the Black American media analyzed for this book, I observed that Gillum was often assigned the hero frame. As a hero is often recognized as a person who embodies characteristics such as courage and is celebrated for a bold approach to problem solving, it is noticeable that, in a Black American media frame, Gillum embodies some of those traits. For example, in one of the first stories in the 2 weeks leading up to election day, in

Afro.com articles "Gillum Surges Ahead in Florida" and "Gillum, DeSantis Exchange Insults in Final Florida Debate," the hero frame is apparent in the coverage of Gillum's suggested campaigning mastery. The first article opens by explaining the lead that Gillum held over his rival, DeSantis: "With about two weeks to go before the midterm elections on Nov. 6, Andrew Gillum, the Democratic candidate for governor of Florida, moved out to a double-digit lead over his Republican rival in a recent poll" (Yoes, 2018, 1).

In the second article that painted a vivid picture of the vitriolic rhetoric between Gillum and DeSantis, the story described Gillum's bold attack against DeSantis, who had won support from President Trump and, according to polls, the majority of registered white men: "My opponent has run this race very, very close to the Trump handbook, where we call each other names, where we run false advertisements" (Spencer & Farrington, 2018).

The Blackcentric media depicted Gillum as a "hero" who could meet sociopolitical and socioeconomic challenges. Gillum's hero frame represented a candidate who would encourage a constituency to believe that he could inspire positivity. The manner in which Gillum's image was depicted was supported in many of the articles that Blackcentric media published about him. Part of the approach allowed Gillum to exude preparation and confidence. An article from TheGrio.com reported Gillum's content on election day.

> Holding his baby son in his arms, and with his two older children at his side, Gillum expressed satisfaction at a campaign he says was run with class and focused on the policy instead of nonsense. "All the way along we tried to talk about the issues that matter to people," Gillum told the press. "People are going out and they're voting for something and not against. And by voting for something, we're returning the politics of decency and what's right and what's common between all of us." (Alford, 2018)

The hero frame suggested that Gillum could not be degraded or frightened by a political rival who had support from the president. The frame also depicted Gillum as ready to defend and conquer opponents. This frame depicted Gillum as a marginalized political competitor who was equipped for victory and not a target who would be defeated easily.

When Blackcentric and Black American media projected the hero frame with a sense of how a candidate fights, it revealed a sense of Gillum's assertiveness. This frame depicted Black leaders as having a contentious relationship with their white colleagues. Gillum's agency was suggested as being assertive and able to defend against fervent political attacks.

Ben Jealous was often portrayed as a peace broker in Blackcentric media. There were very few articles about Jealous, Maryland's formal gubernatorial candidate, in the research window. However, the relatively limited coverage of Jealous' candidacy is very telling. The story "Ben Jealous Wants to Trump Hate in Maryland" had a video component, which could be why this story was only one hundred words in length. Jealous is referred to as a peace broker who wanted to deliver a counternarrative to President Trump's rhetorical style. For example, Terrell Jermaine Starr highlighted Jealous by saying, "Jealous is resilient and believes he can pull off an upset. He wants to make Maryland a state where, under no conditions, a Trump-like atmosphere can develop" (Starr, 2018). The video segment was not analyzed for this study. However, the text version of the story indicated that Starr wanted to frame Jealous as the antithesis to Trump's attitude and rhetoric, which is often described as vapid and mostly divisive.

In an article from Afro.com, Hamil Harris used a framing similar to that found in TheRoot.com articles, saying, "Jealous is hoping to surf a blue wave of Democratic contenders in races across the country, seeking to use political discontent against President Donald Trump to win" (Harris, 2018). This explanation implied that Jealous was expected to act as a "peace broker."

In TheGrio.com's article "Dave Chappelle Supporting Ben Jealous by Making Personal Phone Calls to Maryland Voters," the only online article from TheGrio.com about Ben Jealous during this time period, Cortney Wills reported on the famous comedian's support for Jealous. Chappelle is known for his cutting-edge humor. However, in this article, he was described as a surrogate for Jealous. Wills reported that Chappelle said, "You're on the cusp of having a wonderful governor in the state of Maryland named Ben Jealous" (TheGrio, 2018). Without an explicit endorsement, the text suggested that Jealous was focused more on healing divisions rather than fomenting them.

WHITE-OWNED/MAINSTREAM MEDIA FRAMING

The white-owned media provided a different frame for Abrams, Gillum, and Jealous. Abrams was framed as radical and Gillum was often framed as always awkwardly on the defense. At the same time, however, Jealous was largely ignored. This frame is apparent in the *Washington Times* articles but is also apparent in stories from other mainstream media. For example, the article "Stacy Abrams Admits She Burned Georgia State Flag in College" (Morton, 2018) focused on Abrams's rebellious activism, stating that her rival said that she could not "attempt to rewrite" the past and that he would protect Stone Mountain from "the radical left." Women in politics challenge the radical frame. Many women politicians are forced to walk a thin line to create a constructive, mass-mediated portrayal of a candidate who is socio-politically connected while simultaneously avoiding negative stereotypes of an angry Black woman. Black women candidates are often described as extremists and radicals.

The understanding within this frame is that the radical movement is more about identity and moral sanctimony than ameliorating persisting social problems. The framing of Abrams in mainstream media inferred a presumption that, since there is a contentious election and she is unlike the archetypal white male candidate, the possibility of a moral high ground is hypocritical and illegitimate. For a radical to achieve progress, an evil act must be committed under the guise of prosperity for all. For Abrams, the framing derived from the mainstream news media was that she was attempting to validate her candidacy in the wrong way and was destroying commonly held values.

This is not to say that Abrams was framed as a radical in the conservative *Washington Times* only. The headline from the *New York Times* during the same week, "Stacey Abrams's Burning of Georgia Flag with Confederate Symbol Surfaces on Eve of Debate," indicates that her framing as someone who scoffs at the status quo was thematic throughout the election cycle. NewYorkTimes.com explained Abrams's role in the controversy:

> The protest, which took place around the end of her freshman year at Spelman College in Atlanta, has begun to emerge on social media on the eve of her first debate Tuesday with her Republican opponent, Secretary of State Brian Kemp. Mr. Kemp and his allies have sought to portray her as "too extreme for Georgia." (Fausset, 2018)

Gillum's framing in mainstream media often depicted him as being under attack. The mainstream media focused on the back-and-forth between Gillum and his rival. The following examples illustrate the "on-the-defense" frame and how mainstream media viewed Gillum and his position in the Florida gubernatorial race. For instance, the NewYorkTimes.com article "Text Messages Raise New Questions Over Andrew Gillum's Lobbyist Connections" framed Gillum as a candidate under siege:

> Records made public on Tuesday suggest that Mr. Gillum knowingly accepted a ticket to the Broadway show "Hamilton" from men he believed to be businessmen looking to develop property in Tallahassee—but who were actually undercover F.B.I. agents. (Mazzei, 2018)

Gillum was portrayed as a target of the US government for investigation because he challenged the status quo. This frame also organized a relationship dynamic of how Gillum engaged with the local community; he was in a constant state of war with DeSantis or the federal government and was simultaneously attacked by former president Trump, which was represented in various narratives. Trump perpetually characterized him negatively and criticized his candidacy.

I found no mention of Jealous on the cover pages of mainstream media during the time period studied. This is an indication that Jealous' candidacy was de-emphasized in the mainstream media, unlike the coverage in Afro.co m, TheRoot.com, and TheGrio.com. The lack of coverage of Jealous in the white/mainstream media publications indicates that news stories about other candidates were given preference. This neglect of Jealous' campaign shows a bias in coverage, indicating that his candidacy was not considered as impor-tant to the political fabric as were those of other candidates.

AUTOMATED NEWS MEDIA FRAMING

Knowhere's framing of Abrams was in line with that of the mainstream and white-owned media. Abrams's apparent agency to make her own decisions on the campaign trail was absent. Despite her popularity at the time this research was conducted, the narratives paid closer attention to whom Abrams was affiliated with rather than her own campaign leadership. Knowhere framed Abrams as more focused on shaking up the establishment based on her past than on the idea of a woman equipped with adept leadership qualities. Knowhere stated that "Abrams has been defending herself after a photograph surfaced of her helping to burn the state flag in 1992 as part of a student pro-test because it contained a Confederate emblem" (Knowhere, 2018).

These observations indicate comparisons between what is discussed in the pre-eminent narratives from the mainstream and that from the Blackcentric media. In contrast to Blackcentric media and the automated media source studied here, Abrams was framed as a woman who was fiercely independent and who could handle herself in the challenges posed by political adversaries. In comparison to Blackcentric and mainstream media, the automated article de-emphasized an empowering frame and adopted a frame closer to the radi-cal depiction that was found in the mainstream narratives.

In the automated news article "Trump Attacks Andrew Gillum" there are three variants: left, right, and impartial. In all three versions of the article, the narrative frames Gillum as the embattled candidate. This is one of the few articles with various versions written about Gillum from Knowhere during the researched time period. The article focuses on President Trump and his assessment of Gillum. The first article examined here is the impartial version that Knowhere produced. The only descriptive section in the story that dis-cusses Gillum's race and his slim lead over his competitor:

> Gillum is running to be the first black governor in Florida history. The Florida governor's race is one of the most intensely watched of this campaign cycle. A

RealClearPolitics average of various polls shows Gillum with a 3.2 percentage point lead over DeSantis. (Knowhere, 2018)

Gillum's frustration with media reached its zenith when coverage focused more on alleged corruption than on the candidate's campaigning message. The timing for Gillum was a usual circumstance for Black politicians seeking name recognition. The situation is often challenging for Black politicians as they fight against the establishment. Other studies and polls have shown that Black politicians face fundraising obstacles more often and more seriously than their white counterparts. This can be an even more serious problem for first-time candidates (Solas, 2018).

In the conservative version of this article, Gillum was still viewed as embattled. The article, "Trump Tweets Support for Republican Ron DeSantis in the Florida Gubernatorial Race, Calling Opponent Andrew Gillum a Thief" focused on the president's attack on Gillum (Knowhere, 2018).

Trump posted:

In Florida there is a choice between a Harvard/Yale educated man named @ RonDeSantisFL who has been a great Congressman and will be a great Governor—and a Dem who is a thief and who is Mayor of poorly run Tallahassee, said to be one of the most corrupt cities in the Country! (Knowhere, 2018)

The right-leaning article concentrated on Gillum's shortcomings in the political race rather than on his attributes. It reported that Gillum was the subject of a corruption investigation but that, if he won, he would be the first "African-American governor of Florida" (Knowhere, 2018). The rest of the article described Gillum's acceptance of tickets to a Broadway show from an FBI agent. The article suggested that Gillum was in political trouble. Aside from Gillum's race, the reader cannot learn much about his platform. The information is limited to the candidate's race, the office that he was sought, and the controversy surrounding the situation. If a reader were to look for a cogent explanation of why Gillum was running, it would be nearly impossible to discover.

The "left" article, entitled "Trump Calls Democrat Andrew Gillum 'Thief,' Mayor of 'Corrupt' City," is similar, detailing Gillum's beneficial attributes as a politician and a robust description of his campaign.

On Monday morning, President Donald Trump weighed in on the Florida gubernatorial race with a post attacking the Democratic contender, Tallahassee Mayor Andrew Gillum, as a "thief." In his post , Trump called Gillum's opponent Ron DeSantis a "Harvard/Yale educated man," while calling Gillum a "thief" and "mayor of poorly run Tallahassee" (Knowhere, 2018).

Even with tempered bias in coverage, Knowhere's automated media framing of Gillum depicts him in a disempowering way that aligns with mainstream coverage of him. This dynamic is observable in all three versions of the Knowhere article, left, right, and neutral. The framing of Gillum in automated media was more closely aligned to the white-owned mainstream narratives than to the Blackcentric media. The framing inferences indicate a disproportion among the published media, with some alignment between the mainstream media sources and the automated media source.

Chapter 13

Interrogating Artificial Intelligence in Journalism

The development of questions that supported this research was a key step to produce consistent and relevant conclusions. The following questions increased the likelihood of establishing better connections within the data, especially when considering what data would be collected and how it would be analyzed.

Question 1 calls for exploration of themes in racialized events in the variety of sources of published news articles. Thematic analysis allows for understanding of social phenomena. Using research cues from Cowart et al. (2016), thematic analysis allows for identification of themes among the article examples within a specific time frame.

Question 2 examines consistency among the media to explore agenda-setting inferences shared by conventional US media sources and alternative media sources and how they might share socially suggested constructions with automated news narratives that are algorithmically derived from content on the internet.

Question 3 focuses on placement and use of specific wordage. The adjectives and descriptors are assessed as positive, negative, or neutral. An adjective is considered positive if it refers to positive characteristics of Black candidates. The article headline could be considered negative if a Black person or group is referred to in a derogatory way. If there are no positive or negative ascriptions to the protagonists (or main object of discussion), the article is rated as neutral.

In question 4, I performed an analysis of the texts in news stories to determine whether or how thematic framing was consistent among the publications.

EXAMINING MEDIA IN THE FRAME OF AI

Using framing theory as a theoretical framework, I observed the framing of race during the 2018 US midterm elections as reported by white-owned/ mainstream, Black (Blackcentric) online media, and automated journalism. Borrowing from methodologies used in previous framing and race research, I employed an inductive qualitative method for an efficient assessment of the information. The research was conducted first through a framing analysis and then through a thematic analysis of online print media portraying race during an epoch that many have characterized as a racially polarized nation (Edsall, 2019). "To frame is to select some aspects of a perceived reality and make them more salient in a communicating text, in such a way as to promote a particular problem definition, causal interpretation, moral evaluation, and/ or treatment recommendation" (Entman, 1993, 52). Framing theory guided examination of connections in media coverage of events, people, and/or issues.

The study that I established used a qualitative framing analysis, a method used to analyze how people understand situations and activities, to deliberatively analyze newspaper text and conduct thematic analyses while using a concise method to systematically code article materials. This two-step method was used to examine how top US online mainstream media news outlets, leading Black online news outlets, and a news company that specializes in automated journalism presented issues highlighting race and identity during a US election season.

Framing in text, according to Tankard et al. (1991), can be described as an organizing idea for news content that provides context and suggests the issue through categorization, concentration of specific subject matter, exclusion of unrelated topics, and elaboration on the issue at hand.

This study could assist in understanding how an audience perceives an issue such as race in America, with implications for a society of digitally informative immediacy customized to eliminate biases. Other studies have examined how media frames race, political issues, and candidates, but there is a dearth of empirical research on specific differences in how race is framed during a political season using an automated means of news production via AI algorithms.

Black Americans have experienced marginalization from the mainstream in many areas. This book focuses on specific articles published within a specified time frame to examine the coverage of race in issues and candidates during the US 2018 midterm election season between October 23 and November 6, 2018. The fundamental qualitative study for the book examines dominant frames in the articles from three distinct journalism domains: Blackcentric, mainstream, and automated.

GOALS OF THE INVESTIGATION

This research was not only designed to understand nuances between automated journalism and other forms of mediated communications, with race as the central contextual motif but also as a caveat associated with benign neglect. With changing industry structures incorporating new technologies and increased use of algorithm-based news marketed as AI in news and journalism, there needs to be an investigation of how news is generated and whether it is adversely affecting journalism content regarding issues related to marginalized communities, in this case, Black society.

The encroaching nature of progressive technology use in journalismsuggests the prospect of profound reforms to the operations of the news journalism industry. This research examines how information and issues connected to traditionally excluded communities, such as America's Black society, taken from mainstream discourse, online media, and automated journalism, could influence news and information in that community.

News output is increasing because of the many new digital conduits that are created with the ease of progressive technologies. At the same time, journalism, the art of newsgathering and its dissemination within traditional institutions, is imploding (Twenge et al., 2019). Since newspaper stories, broadcast news, and web-based news are increasingly stored in the cloud and consequently on the internet, they are becoming a large archive. Stories will be accessible at any time in the future. That access will transcend the conventional geographic restrictions imposed by older forms of journalism. Almost instantaneously, search engines show multimedia information on myriad topics. This not only bolsters the impact of journalism for generations to come but also insists on diligent stewardship.

In a digital world of media, the cyclically common transactional communication model between provider and consumer is increasingly quick and more interactive. Audiences are submitting more feedback as their voices are being heard. A wider diversity of stories is being provided. Archives can hold information for extended periods, if not permanently while people are more reactive to the speed with which environmental changes occur in their integrated lives. This adjustment has inspired the use of watch and pocket-sized devices for wearers to consume content at their convenience.

Volumes of journalism archives regarding laws, cultures, customs, and traditions demonstrate that the information derived from journalism is invaluable to the public good. Current narratives will be available for generations of tomorrow. This highlights the necessity for news to reflect various viewpoints not only for accuracy but also to reflect the attitudes and record the actions of participants in the reported community.

As society uses the cloud, the ability to store and access data and programs over the internet to retrieve more information than ever will become more automated. This techno ethos is happening quite rapidly. The progressive move towards automated digital platforming has already been happening within financial news, sports, and basic hard news narratives (Hashem et al., 2015). Journalists will need to adapt to the changes in the environment and safeguard issues of all communities and cultures. With time, the logic of the archive will permeate the consciousness and workflow of journalists. The automation of news production is already happening with the *Washington Post*'s Heliograf system, which selectively builds narratives using AI-driven, algorithm-based technology (Latar, 2018). In the future, journalists will concentrate on interpretation, analysis, and storytelling of more fundamental and impactful changes in society.

Chapter 14

Understanding the Investigative Procedure

In this chapter, we highlight the methodological strategies used to write this book addressing a technological communications intersection. This chapter describes the data collection process, the study design, research questions, the study instrument, the analysis context, and operationalization of terms.

The design of this research is two-fold. The first objective is to improve understanding of themes of race in reporting of people and events during the 2018 midterm election by Black online journalism, mainstream (predominantly white-owned and managed) journalism, and automated journalism (AI-augmented content). The second objective is to examine frames about Black candidates to determine how readers made sense of their candidacies and identities in a narrowcasting and broadcasting hybrid context.

This study relied on two complementary qualitative methods to understand the relationships among the three studied forms of media. To examine and comprehend the textual data in the publications, a research design that looked at content and its contextualization was vital. During the evaluation of data, a thematic analysis was implemented to find themes in the white/mainstream publications, the Blackcentric publications, and the iterations of automated content provided by Knowhere. In the analysis of 272 articles, each was reviewed for content about Black candidates or about racialized issues. Table 14.1 gives a breakdown of the number of stories from each publication. The articles were ascribed themes through thematic analysis and frames through framing analysis. The framing offered a broader perspective for evaluation and analysis. The most frequent emergent themes were considered to be the dominant themes from which the major frames were identified.

The use of framing and thematic methods of analysis was important to understand relationships and attributions related to news narratives. An example is a social media communiqué from the president that captures

Table 14.1   Story Count among Publications

Publication	Count
Afro.com	27
TheGrio.com	40
TheRoot.com	60
TheNewYorkTimes.com	52
TheWashingtonTimes.com	40
USAToday.com	20
Knowhere.com	33
Total	272

national attention. How the mainstream media cover a presidential post and/ or statement in terms of the sourcing material or production bias could determine the output of the narrative in myriad iterations. It cannot be declared with certainty that an article about the presidential post would be widely reported or even featured in generalized media, depending on the article's focus. If it is widely reported, the publication may have its own framing of the post to impart a particular message. Examples of stories that belong across various aggregations are cited in this research. The aim is not to understand the effects of media frames on candidates or to introduce how Black candidates use media frames; thus, focus groups and interviews were not conducted.

OPERATIONAL DEFINITIONS OF CONCEPTS AND TERMS

African Americans: Americans with total or partial ancestry from any of the Black racial groups of Africa. The phrase generally refers to descendants of enslaved Black people in the United States; a similar term is Black American or Afro-American although the latter term is archaic.

Algorithm-driven: an algorithmic process that converts data into a narrative news format with limited to no human intervention except for initial programming managementor at the end for curation.

Automated media: digital media that uses algorithms and AI for news gathering purposes and editorial output

Black Online News Content: news content accessed on the internet usually about Black society and its members examined from a Black-centric perspective

Black: an American having Black African ancestors; African American, negro (archaic). This word is often capitalized because of its recognition of a pan-diasporic identity within North American culture.

Front page or cover page: the first visible page of a newspaper, magazine, or readable publication

Blackcentric: regarding American Black culture as the preeminent narrative

Inner city: the area near the center of a city, often populated with diverse communities and is sometimes associated with social and economic challenges

Minority: a person within a co-cultural group commonly discriminated against in a community, society, or nation based on differences from others including race, religion, language, creed, orientation, or political persuasion

Negro: a member of a group of people originally native to Africa south of the Sahara

Person of color: a person who is non-white or of European parentage

Polisocioeconomic: a portmanteau relating to or concerned with the interaction of political, social, and economic factors at their intersection and synergies

Racialized: narratives possessing a racial tone or characteristics

Salience: the quality of being noticeable or possessing a level of prominence in the minds of the public

Urban: relating to a place and/or area of a city at times connected to Black American spaces

White/mainstream: describing media that provide socially dominant coverage and news narratives; in this research, the term is synonymous with white-owned (non-Black) or mainstream media.

DATA COLLECTION

To address the research questions, I conducted an in-depth framing analysis of seven publications from (a) mainstream media: *USA Today, The Washington Times,* and the *New York Times*; (b) Black, Black American, or Black-centric media: *TheGrio.com, Afro.com,* and *The Root.com*; and (c) automated journalism media: Knowhere's triple article offerings separated by partisan biases and "neutral" perspectives.

All articles were taken from screenshots of the web pages that had been sent to subscribers and posted to the internet from October 23 to November 5, 2018: twenty articles from USAToday.com (*USA Today*), fifty-two articles from NYTimes.com (*The New York Times*), forty articles from WashingtonTimes.com (*Washington Times*), twenty-seven articles from Afro.com (*The Afro*), forty articles from TheGrio.com, sixty articles from TheRoot.com, and thirty-three articles from KnowhereNews.com (Knowhere), for a total of nearly three hundred articles. The articles were culled from the Lexis Nexis database and from online sources using the internet to access the publications' websites. LexisNexis, published online news articles, and disseminated e-newsletters (email newsletters) served as the method to obtain newspaper articles because they were easily accessible and had an expanse of data. Only articles relating to candidates of color were examined.

USA Today has an international distribution that serves a range of market sizes in the United States. This publication, which has a traditional newspaper format and online format, is regarded as having a centrist audience. It is influenced by the styles of local, regional, and national newspapers. It has a digital subscriber base of more than a half million people and a weekly print circulation of more than 700,000. According to research statistics, *USA Today* has a daily readership of more than 2.5 million people (marketing.usatoday.com, 2017). *USA Today* has the largest circulation of any newspaper; it is distributed in all fifty states and the District of Columbia.

The New York Times is one of the top daily newspapers in the United States. For five days a week in 2017, the average weekday circulation was more than 500,000. It also has one of the largest weekend distributions, 1,438,585 (Feldman, 2019). *The New York Times* also possesses worldwide distribution. This publication focuses on newspaper and online reports of international news events, as well as regional and national events. Through comprehensive coverage of national and international news, it produces more information than other newspapers (Ulrich's Periodicals Directory, 2019). Carragee (2019) wrote that *The New York Times* focuses attention on international politics and has a substantive influence on American political discourse because of its ability to reach elites who are considered to be decision makers.

The Washington Times is a popular and influential paper in the United States. Its headquarters are in the nation's capital, the center of politics. Its major daily edition is distributed throughout the District of Columbia and in parts of Maryland and Virginia. This paper was examined in this research because of its national distribution and its coverage of the US government at the highest levels. It is also a publication of source material for Knowhere, the center of this case study of automated journalism. The leading stories of this paper are often covered in television and radio news programs and provide content for late-night talk show formats that shape the zeitgeist.

The Afro is the truncated name of the *Afro-American*. The internet-based component of *The Afro-American*, afro.com, has been a proponent of "racial equality and economic advancement for Black Americans for 125 years" (Afro.com, 2023). *The Afro* was chosen for this research because of its national position for reporting on issues that are important to Black society and its communities. It is a Black-owned and operated publication. *The Afro* has a circulation in several predominantly Black communities across the country, which has enabled it to engage deeply with Black society on a profound and national scale.

TheGrio.com is a website based in New York City. It shares news, entertainment, and video content to appeal to an "African American" audience (Kee, 2009). This website started in 2009 as a division of NBC News. Because of its Black American content, it discusses issues in the Black community in more depth than do its commercial competitors, who tend to cater to the status quo. According to SimilarWeb.com, most of *TheGrio*'s audience searches the website for developing news items in comparison to entertainment and technology posts. It is estimated that this website achieves nearly 1.5 million visitors a month. Its rank is 13,549 among leading websites in the United States, according to SimilarWeb.com (2023).

TheRoot.com provides news and supports the shares of "thought-leaders and influencers" throughout the country (The Root Staff, 2016). It is considered to be a premier site for news, opinions, and culture for the African American population. This site welcomes approximately 6.5 million unique monthly visits. Like the Afro.com and TheGrio.com, TheRoot.com provides content that examines Black American culture and experiences deriving from the Diaspora more than other web-based content that is broader in nature and more inclusive of the white community. TheRoot.com is currently ranked 1,438 among websites in the United States, according to SimilarWeb.com (2023).

Knowhere is a San Francisco- and London-based news publication. This website focuses on news narratives that it derives from algorithms that scour or "scrub" the internet for content. Company executives consider their proprietary form of AI as a way to mitigate biases that are consequently considered to be invasive in today's media world. Knowhere's creators say that the website was created in part due to the claims that there is a rise of "fake news," a term popularized by the forty-fifth President of the United States, President Donald J. Trump, who expressed dissatisfaction with perceived political partisanship in published and broadcast news narratives. Knowhere's newsletter states that it is "a response to today's proliferation of biased narratives, misinformation, and echo-chambers. With the support of Knowhere's machine learning technology, the company's editorial team is free to uncover and dive into the factual elements of a story" (KnowhereNews.com, 2019). So far, this has been the only web-based news site that uses a form of AI and algorithms to produce hard news and political news on a daily basis except for weekends, but other computer-based platforms have been emerging to the forefront. Knowhere's content heavily focuses on topics du jour but has not been exclusive to politics, sometimes creating other opportunities to crossover into accessing entertainment and sports news.

Knowhere has devoted its expertise in utilizing algorithms and ANI to using non-human-produced or -manipulated material except for the news narrative created by the end of the curation process. This is what makes this company unique in its distribution of news in contrast to other companies that use automated technologies in limited amounts, such as the Associated Press (Associated Press, 2018). The Knowhere articles were found in published triplicates: "Left," "Right," and "Neutral." When Knowhere's algorithms comb the internet for trending articles, the publishers of those articles are ranked by level of trustworthiness based on an algorithm. The more trustworthy the source, the greater position in the hierarchy the news story is shown and the more likely that the algorithm will extract data from it. Knowhere's AI-powered algorithms pick up stories from the *Washington Post* and myriad other sources to write news narratives. While the *Washington Post* is often cited by Knowhere, it is not always considered the pre-eminent news source.

Chapter 15

Behind the Research

RESEARCH QUESTION 1

Research question 1 sought to identify the themes emerging from racialized events that mention Black candidates during the 2018 US midterm elections. For this question, the automated news source was directly compared to the traditional media sources. The examination resulted in four emergent themes, focused on the Black experience and its ties to the political election process. This is to be expected because of the time frame of this research, during an election year. The stories presented narratives focused on connections to the Black experience. Word clouds were constructed to understand the verbiage used to describe events and politicians. Although there were several thematic similarities in the data, only the dominant themes connecting to Black candidates and the Black experience were categorized for coding. A thematic map shown in figure 15.1 is designed to show how content is sorted by categories into themes. The textual analysis of the data indicated themes and patterns. After a thorough review of the framing of Black political candidates and deliberative coding, the major themes were identified as racial division, Black polisocioeconomic struggle, voter suppression, and Black empowerment.

RACIAL DIVISION

Mentions of political candidates addressing racial division was apparent. Publications referred to candidates weighing in on sensitive social topics. One of the prominent stories during the target time was the blackface controversy involving the popular former Fox News Network anchor, Megyn Kelly.

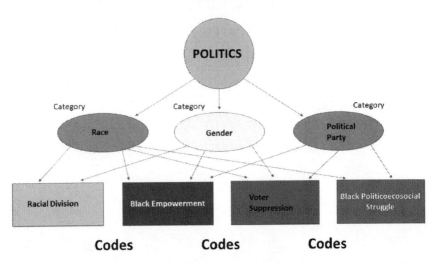

Figure 15.1   How Categories and Themes Are Separated for Later Qualitative Coding

Political candidates offered perspectives on the controversy, but overall, the media covered the story with a focus on front and cover pages.

In the white/mainstream publication, the *New York Times*, the article "Blackface Remarks by Megyn Kelly Lead to Rift with NBC" described the controversy as ostensibly divisive along color lines, writing:

> On Wednesday's "Today" show, the NBC anchor Craig Melvin called her comments "racist and ignorant," and Al Roker, the usually genial weatherman, said that Ms. Kelly "owes a bigger apology to folks of color around the country." The MSNBC anchor Jacob Soboroff wrote on Twitter that her remarks were "vile." (Koblin & Grynbaum, 2018, 3)

The topic was frequently discussed in the Blackcentric news sources. All three Blackcentric publications featured stories about Kelly's blackface drama as she questioned whether the tradition was racist and why. TheRoot .com discussed Kelly's showcased ignorance and the historical context of the issue:

> On the Tuesday morning episode of her talk show, *Megyn Kelly TODAY*, Kelly once again showed her complete lack of cultural awareness when she claimed blackface had once been "OK" when she was younger (Kai, 2018, 1). TheGrio .com posted a similar take on the story, condemning Kelly's query.

"But what is racist?" Kelly pondered on *Megyn Kelly Today* to a panel that included Jenna Bush Hager, Jacob Soboroff, and Melissa Rivers. "You truly do get in trouble if you are a white person who puts on blackface at

Halloween or a black person who puts on whiteface for Halloween" (Ruiz, 2018). Consistent in the Blackcentric media publications was the propensity to discuss the history of blackface and how it had been a part of American entertainment for decades and the events leading up to this embrace of bastardized Black cultural expression. The historical breakdown ostensibly catered to a predominately Black audience by presenting more context to the issue. In offering some historical comprehension, these news organizations put a spotlight on challenges and successes in Black society while providing a nuanced approach to the lives of Black Americans. The following is how Knowhere described the occurrence.

> NBC pulled Megyn Kelly off the air Thursday, one day after she apologized for making racially insensitive comments about the use of blackface. NBC is reportedly weighing options for Kelly's future at the network. On Tuesday's episode of her show, "Megyn Kelly Today," Kelly seemed to question whether it was wrong to wear blackface, sparking an immediate backlash. (Knowhere, 2018)

Knowhere's narrative on the blackface issue was similar to that of other media that focused on Kelly's shortcomings regarding cultural awareness rather than including the history of blackface or, additionally, those who may have been offended by Kelly's query that shocked many because of her blatant ignorance of cultural awareness and emotional intelligence. The persistence of blackface as a stereotype in American media was not new and had a deep historical presence throughout the twentieth century, continuing even today when members of the white public use blackface for intimidation or to dress up on Halloween.

Historic minstrelsy performed in blackface mocked African American oral traditions, physiognomy, dress, dance, and song. By masquerading in blackface, whites objectified African American life experiences while at the same time downplaying Black Americans' cultural contributions and relevance. From the viewpoint of an assimilative gaze, blackface minstrelsy allowed whites to take pleasure in the "hostile or sexual aggressiveness" of Blacks while the white race escaped the harm; in a way that such dramas assigned to the African American community were perpetuated (Reid, 1993, 5).

The topic of blackface has global implications in the media and was relevant enough for the automated news publication to report on it.

The critique of cultural influence is evaluated in all forms of communication. For example, a criticism of cultural transference is framed through the treatment of racial bias, discrimination, stereotyping, and prejudice. Central aspects regarding the comprehension of racial bias in media sit at the intersection of cultural connectivity. As Janell Hobson (2008) posited, "Representations of digital technology recreate social and cultural hierarchies that encourage appropriation and colonization of knowledge and bodies from marginal communities" (113).

BLACK POLISOCIOECONOMIC STRUGGLE

Another theme in the studied publications was polisocioeconomic struggle. Although the naming of this category is arcane, it could be described as the incorporation of themes that include racially insensitive reinforcements of persistent tropes. The etymological assignment is a portmanteau to categorize the sociopolitical and socioeconomic fora that address class and the efforts of Black self-determinism. This description sits at the intersection of cultural adversity for members of the Black community in America that affect the population politically and economically. This could include stereotypes, economic exclusion, political adversity, and other domains that, in combination, describe a multilayered effect of white oppression in control over a co-cultural Black American population. Several publications discussed the ramifications of growing public divisions that many believed were exacerbated by President Trump, with adverse effects on the Black American experience.

Throughout the studied period, the issue of blackface was pre-eminent in news articles and coverage. An article in *The New York Times* highlighted this theme as "Megyn Kelly Apologizes for Blackface Comments." In this article, the Black experience of being dehumanized was recapitulated in a discussion about blackface when the anchor of the *Today* show, Kelly, said that she did not understand why blackface was offensive. Kelly, who was forty-seven at the time, was old enough to know the political, social, and economic repercussions of generations of the US white majority accepting blackface as a form of entertainment. Blackface, the minstrel act of a white person painting their face black to imitate Black people, had been an entertainment staple in the nineteenth century. However, with its performative acceptance largely relegated to the socially unaware, it is widely understood to be offensive. Yet still, Kelly expressed surprise over the controversy in the article "Megyn Kelly's 'Blackface' Remarks Leave Her Future at NBC in Doubt" in NewYorkTimes.com. Kelly was cited as saying about the American pastime that was demeaning to the Black community,

> "What is racist?" Ms. Kelly asked. "You do get in trouble if you are a white person who puts on blackface on Halloween, or a black person who puts on whiteface for Halloween. Back when I was a kid, that was O.K., as long as you were dressing up as a character." (Koblin & Grynbaum, 2018)

The theme is continued in several *USA Today* articles but was popular in the other white/mainstream publication *USA Today*'s "Megyn Kelly Was

Making Racist Comments Long Before 'Blackface.' NBC hired her anyway."
This article highlights the polisocioeconomic struggle of Black Americans as
it reported Kelly's stereotyping of Black men:

> That the black community suffered from a "thug mentality" where "it's cool to
> sort of hate the cops and hang out—and be somebody who doesn't necessarily
> prize being there for your family." (Powers, 2018)

The Washington Times also addressed this theme in the story, "Candace
Owens pushes 'Blexit' campaign: 'No group . . . more taken advantage of
by the Democrats'" quoting Owens, a Black conservative activist, as saying, "There is no group in America that has been more lied to, more abused,
or more taken advantage of by the Democrats than black people" (Morton,
2018). The article expressed feelings of exploitation of America's Black society by the Democratic party. Despite this publication's conservative bias, the
theme of the polisocioeconomic struggle that is part of the Black experience
in America was often discussed throughout the studied period in articles such
as "Democratic Sen. Joe Donnelly Mocked for Praising Minority Staffers'
Work Ethic," which challenged Black employees' experience in the workplace. Donnelly is reported as saying this about two non-white employees:

> "Our state director is Indian American, but he does an amazing job," he said.
> "Our director of all constituent services, she's African-American, but she does
> an even more incredible job than you could ever imagine." (Chasmar, 2018)

The polisocioeconomic theme was bolder in Blackcentric media than in
the other publication types. Afro.com, for example, featured numerous stories
about the issue of Megyn Kelly and blackface, with many Black celebrities
and broadcast journalism leaders such as Al Roker speaking out. The polisocioeconomic theme was also exhibited in other articles from Afro.com,
such as "Police: Armed White Man Confronts Black GOP Volunteer," which
pointed to the challenging rigors that Black Americans face doing ostensibly
pedestrian things. This story was also featured in the Associated Press, which
was prominently featured prominently on the Afro.com website describing
the experience of a Black Republican volunteer:

Volunteer Derek Partee told *The News & Observer* that three white people
angrily approached him Wednesday at a poll in Charlotte. He posted pictures
of the people on Facebook, saying they were calling him racial slurs and
threatening him (Associated Press, 2018).

The accosted person, Derek Partee, told police, "They didn't care whether
I was a Democrat or a Republican, they just cared that I was Black" (Associated Press, 2018).

TheRoot.com shared the polisocioeconomic theme in its story "Bank Exec Slammed for Dressing as Kanye in Blackface with MAGA hat" (Morgan-Smith, 2018). TheRoot.com reported that Bryan Lenertz, a banking executive, decided to post pics dressed as Kanye West by painting his face brown, throwing on a MAGA hat, shades, and a camouflage coat to imitate the aesthtic of the award-winning musician. To complete the look, Lenertz's wife reportedly dressed as West's wife Kim Kardashian (Morgan-Smith, 2018).

This story combines the social and economic implications of racial adversity in America. TheGrio.com presented this theme with other stories on blackface and another story about Al Roker being blamed for "whiteface" as he vehemently rebuked racist accusations.

TheGrio.com also featured the story "Black Doctor Claims She Was Racially Profiled on a Delta Flight to Boston." This story described the challenges a Black doctor faced when trying to help a passenger in distress while the flight attendant doubted and questioned her credentials and expertise. Dr. Stanford told CNN that even though she was eventually allowed to help the passenger, who was deemed to be having a panic attack and feeling claustrophobic, the constant badgering of the Black woman about her medical background was believed to be "100 percent racially biased" (Telusma, 2018). This theme was also reflected in the automated news sample.

The Knowhere article "Georgia Gubernatorial Race" points to the polisocioeconomic struggle that Abrams faced as a gubernatorial candidate. Despite challenging Secretary of State Brian Kemp for the governorship and even though Kemp was overseeing elections, Abrams was chided by Vice-President Mike Pence for having celebrities bolster her credibility as a potential statesman representing all of Georgia. The article focused on comedian Will Ferrell, talk show host and media mogul Oprah Winfrey, and dissenting Vice President Pence. "I heard Oprah is in town today," Pence said during a rally in Dalton on Thursday. "I got a message for all of Stacey Abrams's liberal Hollywood friends: This ain't Hollywood!" (Knowhere, 2018). Abrams's struggle for relevance was challenged in this article. While the article did not discuss much about Abrams's candidacy, it alluded to the struggle that Abrams and those whom she represented faced:

> "I am here today because of Stacey Abrams," Winfrey said. "I am here today because of the men and because of the women who were lynched, who were humiliated, who were discriminated against, who were suppressed, who were repressed and oppressed for the right for the equality at the polls." (Knowhere, 2018)

The polisocioeconomic theme encompasses not just issues of income inequality, political stagnation, and education; it assumes occupational status and perceptions of social status and class. As shown in white/mainstream media samples and Blackcentric samples, relevant themes characterizing the human experience can include quality of life ascriptions, including opportunities and privileges given to people in a society. This thematic arrangement is also found in the automated journalism sample, which characterizes the combination of socioeconomic and sociopolitical factors that America's Black community experiences.

VOTER SUPPRESSION

In Knowhere's article "Democratic Leaders Criticize Trump After Attempted Bombings," the focus on voter suppression is taken from the headlines of that day (Knowhere, 2018). Looking first at Blackcentric media, an Afro.com article epitomized the struggle that Black candidates face in US politics. The "Georgia Election Fight Shows That Black Voter Suppression Still Flourishes" is written from the perspective of the white male in the story, not the person of focus, Stacey Abrams.

> Georgia's Republican Secretary of State Brian Kemp has been sued for suppressing minority votes after an Associated Press investigation revealed a month before November's midterm election that his office has not approved 53,000 voter registrations—most of them filed by African Americans. (Knight, 2018)

This story could have been written from the perspective of Abrams, whom the story was referencing. Instead, the Knowhere story adopted a similar theme to that the mainstream sources. The story depicted Abrams as an embattled candidate embroiled in a political struggle, needing to resort to litigious methods to be competitive. Abrams never discussed her platform in the article, which presumably was written to focus on why her political path seemed fraught with obstacles. However, that particular nuanced narrative was missing in the automated journalism article despite being discussed in Grio.com and TheRoot.com.

The mainstream media publications also discussed themes of voter suppression. This article from the *Courier Journal*, part of the *USA Today* network, discussed voter suppression in this way regarding the state of Kentucky as it strategized to influence election outcomes by discouraging or restricting certain groups of people from voting.

> States are purging registration rolls and passing voter suppression laws that restrict early voting, limit forms of acceptable identification and—as is the shameful case in Kentucky—block people with felony convictions from

regaining their right to vote, even after they have paid the penalty for their crimes. (Morgan, 2018, 1)

TheWashingtonTimes.com presented themes of Black empowerment in a different way. An article that featured conservative activist Candace Owens quoted her in a thematic expression of empowerment through a mass exodus of Black involvement in the Democratic party called Blexit.

In a weekend column for Breitbart News, she described Blexit as "a national movement of minorities that has awakened to the truth. It is for those who have taken an objective look at our decades-long allegiance to the left and asked ourselves, what do we have to show for it?" (Morton, 2018).

Knowhere exhibited the theme of voter suppression in two stories published during the study period. Former US President Jimmy Carter weighed in on the race between Stacey Abrams and Brian Kemp for the Georgia governorship. Carter appealed to the GOP candidate to step down from his position as Secretary of State to preserve the integrity of the gubernatorial race, since Kemp was the acting steward of elections over the gubernatorial race in which he was a candidate. Knowhere covered this story called "Jimmy Carter Calls for Brian Kemp to Resign" reporting,

The letter is the latest turn in an election in which the closing month is being defined by Democrats' accusations of attempted voter suppression and Republicans' countercharges of attempted voter fraud. (Knowhere, 2018)

Another Knowhere article about voter suppression labeled as "impartial," "Kemp Opens Probe into Democrats Over 'Cyberattack' Ahead of Election" takes the perspective of the mainstream and highlights Kemp's allegations of voter registration hacking.

Georgia's Republican gubernatorial candidate and Secretary of State Brian Kemp said Sunday that his office had launched a probe into the state's Democratic Party, accusing it of trying to hack Georgia's voter registration system without providing evidence of the allegation. (Knowhere, 2018, para. 1)

Knowhere's left-leaning version of this same story indicates a bias for the mainstream perspective. Once again, even as Abrams represented the liberal or left-leaning candidate, the story focused on Kemp's accusations and outrage:

Kemp alleged that the state Democratic Party undertook "a failed attempt to hack the state's voter registration system" and said his office had alerted the FBI and Department of Homeland Security. His office declined to provide any details of the alleged hacking attempt, which Democratic officials have strongly denied. (Knowhere, 2018, para. 3)

This excerpt was taken from the third paragraph of the story. Out of seven paragraphs, only the last paragraph, the seventh, mentioned Abrams's candidacy, using half of the paragraph to discuss her race.

The right-leaning version of this story focused heavily on Kemp's version of accounts leading to his accusations of Democrat voter registration hacking. The story called "Investigation Launched into Georgia Democrats Over Hacking" also discussed the possibility of Democrats being involved in cybercrimes. While the other articles did not go into depth about Abrams's status in the race, this article stated that "Kemp is also the Republican gubernatorial candidate and enjoys a slight lead over his Democratic opponent, Stacey Abrams" (Knowhere, 2018). From the three iterations of Knowhere's accounts regarding voter suppression, this theme focused heavily on the white male candidate's perspectives and grievances more than those of his rivals. Because this story was dominant in the headlines, it took on a level of importance with Knowhere, as well. The Knowhere articles gave the allegations a spotlight, suggesting the importance of this theme.

In Blackcentric media, the theme of voter suppression was interwoven with other stories highlighting the Black experience of campaigning whilst a highly polarized voter electorate. TheRoot.com, for example, featured prominent stories such as "Voter Suppression Is Real and It Really Affects Black People" (Johnson, 2018) and "Black Voters in Georgia Say Something Funny Is Going on With Their Voting Machines" (Harriot, 2018). Other stories, such as "White Woman Calls the Cops on Black Woman for Canvassing in Wealthy Neighborhood," demonstrated how serious the problem of voter suppression seemed to be during the Georgia election. TheRoot.com seemed to prioritize the theme of voter suppression more than other themes and issues of focus in other media studied for this research.

BLACK EMPOWERMENT

As would be expected, Black empowerment occupied a thematic presence throughout the published media. The quest for Black Americans to have access to more property and capital was alluded to in several stories in anticipation of Black candidates winning their respective races. Black empowerment is a common theme in publications that focus on justice within Black culture.

Black Nationalism is characterized by a focus on Black empowerment, economic independence, and a heightened awareness of Black history and culture.

Its goal is to acknowledge and honor the dignity and humanity of Black people. (Fredrickson, 1996)

In mainstream media, the Black empowerment theme was noticeable in several articles. This particular article from the *New York Times* discussed Mike Espy, who was running for a strongly contended US Senate seat in Mississippi.

"People are tired of the reality show in Washington," he said at the Democratic dinner in Greenville, without naming the president. "It diverts attention from the real problems we see every day: the rural hospitals that are closing, the prescription drugs that are still too high, the pre-existing conditions that sap our strength." (Fandos, 2018, para. 1)

Although Espy was not mentioned often during the time period of this research, the way *The New York Times* mentioned the former Senatorial candidate is notable. The article focused on the promises that Espy wanted to bring to disadvantaged Black communities so members could be a larger part of US economic success. The coverage surrounding Espy also focused on racial identity in Mississippi, where he was often ignored or maligned. The other major theme in his news narrative included Espy's proclamations that he believed that Mississippians deserved to have access to good-paying jobs. Other articles suggested that he was adhering to principles that he described in his support of the Black Economic Alliance. He declared that he wanted to create policies that would level the playing field for Black communities.

The New York Times also published a story about Stacey Abrams. The story, entitled "Stacey Abrams, a Daughter of the South, Asks Georgia to Change," discussed Abrams as a rising star who hoped to empower the Black community through her leadership, should she be elected governor. This story was published with a diverging narrative while contemporaneously other stories focused on Abrams's subversive activities. This quotation combined both her desire to challenge the status quo and embrace a Black empowerment agenda.

Out of the student upheavals, she and others founded a new group, Students for African American Empowerment, or SAAE. The Rev. Otis Moss III, an early member, said it represented an array of ideologies, while the Rev. Lukata Mjumbe, another member and now a pastor in New Jersey, said it was part of the continuum of civil rights activism on black college campuses, influenced by groups like the Student Nonviolent Coordinating Committee and the Black Panther Party. (Lyall & Fausset, 2018, para. 1)

In another *Washington Times* article, "If House Leaders Change, Black Dems Want 1 of 2 Top Posts," Louisiana Democratic Representative Cedric Richmond spoke out on the need for more Black leadership in Congress.

Louisiana Democratic Re Cedric Richmond wrote colleagues Thursday that despite the party's "celebration of diversity," a black lawmaker has never held one of the two top jobs. The Louisiana lawmaker adds, "It's time we walk our talk." (Associated Press, 2018, para. 2)

Blackcentric media also contained themes of Black empowerment in the quest for equality. The story "Fight for . . . Who We Are" quoted Democrat California Senator Kamala Harris.

Harris acknowledged the importance of black voters in South Carolina and Democratic politics generally. The senator compared current national tensions to the civil rights era, describing her parents as active in that movement. She quipped that voters "can honor the ancestors with absentee ballots," rather than waiting until Election Day (Barrow & Kinnard, 2018).

The story from Afro.com discussed how Harris connected with women who were victims of sexual violence. One woman was brought to tears when she met Ms. Harris, saying, "The way she addressed her was empowering for women who have never told their stories. . . . I didn't tell mine until this year" (as cited in Barrow & Kinnard, 2018, para. 1).

Knowhere continued the Black empowerment theme in its story. Music artist Pharrell Williams issued a cease and desist letter to President Trump, barring the president from using his song "Happy" for campaign rallies. The letter barred Trump from using any of his music without permission. The president's campaign used the song on the same day that the country was grieving an anti-Semitic mass shooting at a Pittsburgh synagogue. Williams's attorney, Howard King, wrote the letter. King's letter noted that if the president continued to play the song at his rallies, it would violate copyright and trademark laws (Knowhere, 2018). This story was covered by *The Washington Times* and *USA Today* in a similar fashion, alluding to Williams's reclamation of his music from the most powerful political figure in the nation.

RESEARCH QUESTION 2

Research question 2 examined whether themes were consistent among all three publication styles while searching for thematic consistency among the studied publications. The text necessitated a deep analysis to determine whether any thematic framing used in these publications was consistent among the three types of publications. I found consistent treatments among the three publication types. Shared themes indicated similarity in the mainstream and Blackcentric journalism. This is to be expected because of the way Knowhere culls news from trending and popular news stories online.

The similarities in the themes were examined by identifying recurring references. If a reference was made more than once, it was noted. Themes that were mentioned more than twice were weighed more heavily for final consideration. For example, if a publication discussed an issue regarding race in the context of voting, it was counted as separate to a reference to race within a socioeconomic struggle. Each article that mentioned race was placed in the context of the discussion of race. For example, in the story regarding volunteer Derek Partee, the story could have inserted a narrative on voter suppression. However, Partee was not voting at the time nor was he registering voters. Therefore, the article fit into a different category regarding race and politics and class, looking at a behavior of hegemonic intimidation at the core of the event leading to Partee's victimization.

The scrutiny of the presented narratives focused on the context of the thematic connections, rather than the number of mentions of a specific subject. This directed the research to better understand in more intricate ways how these publications present certain themes that were then measured for their substantive relevance within a framing analysis.

The results indicated that themes consistent throughout the publications supported Knowhere's means of deriving its content from the internet. This was to be expected, based on Knowhere's narrative production model. In reference to collective consistencies, Knowhere uses other publications outside of the examples shown solely in this research. Of the seven units of analysis that were used in this research, the strength of the four themes indicates similar inferences between what the most widely read publications rendered versus what Knowhere aggregated and diversified in its content. Collectively, there were some thematic consistencies in how racial events were presented and discussed, but there were also dissimilarities, discussed in the next paragraphs.

SUBTHEMES

Historic Racism

This section of the results for research question 2 is important because of themes that were present in the publications but did not coincide on all media platforms. These sub-themes are important because of the similarity of the automated media example to the white/mainstream media sample but the lack of similarity to the Blackcentric media sample.

One theme that the Blackcentric media covered that seemed to be neglected by the white/mainstream media and automated media was the contextualization of historic racism. Three Blackcentric publications, Grio.com, Theroot.com, and Afro.com, covered the story about the domestic terrorist Cesar Sayoc,

Jr., and how it connected with historic racism and intimidation practices. This intimidation in a political election cycle was not just about voting, but about the very notion of Black people being politically engaged and simultaneously being challenged by those who try to deter those efforts. In the story entitled "55 Years Ago, Someone Blamed a Bombing on a Racist Politician" from TheRoot.com, "Pipe Bombs Aimed at Several Trump Political Targets Alarms Nation at Highly Divisive Time" from Thegrio.com, and "Bomb Scare Rattles Those Touched by Past Political Violence" from Afro.com, they described incidents in which Sayoc Jr. intended specifically to scare or harm Black people. They described the incidents as part of a tradition of racist history that has become interwoven into the Black experience in America. This theme of historic racism was only marginally covered in the white/mainstream media samples and was largely ignored by the automated media data sample. The story was covered only once in the studied two weeks, without the historic contextualization found throughout the Blackcentric media.

Black Civic Engagement

In TheRoot.com's story "Black College Students in Florida Use Early Voting to Make Sure Their Voices Will Be Taken Seriously," there is a focus on Black civic engagement in the political process. In the Blackcentric media, there were several references or suggestions regarding civic engagement. TheRoot.c om offered this theme most clearly in a story written by Terrell Jermaine Starr:

> Getting students involved in the electoral process has always been central to the college's mission of civic engagement, said Marie Health, director of the Schell-Sweet center. We like to have positive engagement in our civic and public affairs and to incorporate the community in a way that we can enhance their education, as well as their community development. (Starr, 2018, para. 1)

TheGrio.com described the action of civic engagement for Black Americans in the story "Reaching Millennials and Young Voters with Education, Entertainment." This story described how, from social media campaigns to day parties and videos, creative ways were used to get younger Black citizens engaged for the 2018 midterm elections. The events were targeted toward Millennials and Generation Z voters to get them to the polls on November 6th. The efforts included focused outreach to young African American voters.

> At many Historically Black Colleges and Universities (HCBUs) nationwide, voter engagement is in full swing. Among them is Morgan State University in Baltimore, where a national organization called Black Girls Vote, Inc. recently launched its first collegiate chapter on the campus. (Owens, 2018)

News stories that concentrated on Black civic engagement were not covered as extensively in the other media samples. This neglect indicates a depriori- tization by the white/mainstream media and the automated media format that ostensibly takes its cues from the dominant and omnipresent established media. The inconsistencies between the Blackcentric media and the automated journalism example could be explained by relationships between what the algorithms discover and categorize in comparison to the wealth of informa- tion provided by the publications that propagate content on the internet. A general analysis revealed these inconsistencies because of the specific content that the automated content publishes. An examination of the analyzed publica- tion texts suggested a process of the automated media content to more closely mirror the white/mainstream publications. In an analysis of the published content, I found profound thematic comparisons in the pattern of relation- ships between the researched publications. Of course, there is an expecta- tion of similarities between established media and the emergent media, as it models some of its content from the established media. However, what is also revealed is the number of themes that the automated media neglects.

RESEARCH QUESTION 3

Research question 3 referenced how did the Blackcentric, white-owned, and automated publications use article/headline descriptors and article placement/ length regarding Black candidates during the 2018 US midterm elections? This research question was designed to determine how Blackcentric, white-owned, and automated publications used article/headline descriptors and article place- ment/length regarding Black candidates during the 2018 US midterm elections on the covers and front pages of their respective websites. I found differences in where the headlines were placed by the various media. There were dispari- ties in article length among the media. Knowhere tended to present shorter articles because of its format. Technologies using NLP and large language models have mostly centered on experimentation. The way that language is used to describe specific events can sometimes be hit or miss with its accuracy, a nod to the complexities and context necessary for fully understanding mes- saging. Knowhere's brevity in headline generation with less detail broadens interpretation and susceptibility to misinterpreted comprehension.

RESEARCH QUESTION 4

Research question 4 was, what are the differences in the framing of Black candidates between Blackcentric, white-owned, and automated publications during the 2018 midterm election? Differences in how publications framed Black candidates were evident. The three major candidates, Stacey Abrams, Andrew Gillum, and Ben Jealous, were all covered through the more conventional media sources. In several cases, the frames used by mainstream/white-owned media were similar to frames used by automated media. The indications highlighted that there was much more nuance used in the Black-centric media about the specific candidates studied versus the continued tropes that were perpetuated in the mainstream. These observations were consistent with previous media critiques that examine racial disparities in news narrative expression.

Media coverage that could be racially biased has been a large component that has contributed to unreliable and disparate outcomes in media portrayals. News media that is not monitored for unbalanced coverage often reinforces the tropes associated with certain marginalized groups. The differences in framing outline the need for media to be more deliberate in their way of decreasing racially biased narratives stemming from inconsistent or incomplete reporting.

SUMMARY OF THE RESULTS

The fast-paced development of AI technologies is undoubtedly changing the means of production in many newsrooms in the United States and even in ways that we may not have realized yet (Farber, 2017). The use of automated journalism with its foundation in ANI controlling and utilizing the deployment of algorithms is an aspect that will increasingly become a part of journalism's means of production. As this study demonstrates, intersectional relationships between mainstream/white-owned journalism and the mirroring of content in the automated journalism format can be inferred. There was a weaker relationship between the Blackcentric media and the automated media in their framing of Black candidates and Black experiences. Figure 15.2 displays a glimpse of Knowhere's process when collating content from other news publications before creating its own news narrative versions. Editors involved in the process attempt to create two versions of a story with one bias that leans to the right, the other to the left, and a third impartial version.

Currently, the pursuit of AI technology in journalism is unregulated in its incipient stages. If left unmonitored, AI in journalism could pose a threat to democracy when accounting for diverse representations and viewpoints of the public. This threat is exacerbated by the increase in ethnically diverse candidates and their political platforms. Journalists, editors, producers, engineers, and media gatekeepers must pay attention to be innovative and

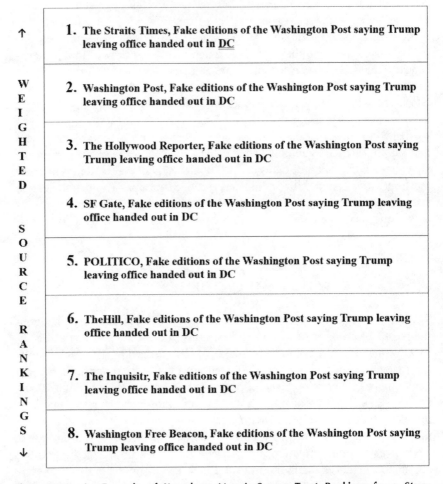

Home   Breaking News Timeline   Archive   Share

Sources   Other Reporting   Primary

Figure 15.2   An Example of Knowhere News's Source Trust Rankings for a Story Regarding Fake Editions of the *Washington Post* Handed Out at Multiple Locations in Washington, DC

forward-thinking in AI journalism so that this emerging technology is more inclusive and less biased, even if unintentional.

If Knowhere is to be a model of automated general news narrative development that eliminates biases because it is one of very few publications specializing in this area, more diverse data is needed to improve output. Automated journalism sources are not influenced by implications or interpretations of framing. Humans still lead this sentient nuance in comparison to machines when reporting news. By engaging in better data collection practices, media business leaders can provide better services to information seekers on a more granular level. Media artificial intelligence is expected to adopt more content personalization. Although there can be a tendency of disparate storytelling because of partisan bias, there is still bias by omission regarding narratives that would allow for a fuller framing of the subject of the article.

As observed in this research, there are various social constructions of meanings, some of which are shared in the way the mainstream media present themes and frame issues related to the Black experience and the way that Knowhere presents those themes and frames. There are conspicuous differences between Knowhere and Blackcentric media in the way that details are prioritized; in a manner that could be considered more progressive in its expression in Blackcentric media, while in the automated mode, coverage is more narratively insipid. As described, Knowhere takes its information from already established stories and reconstitutes messaging to produce more nuanced narrative content.

In numerous ways, AI is already being used in some of the largest newsrooms in the country. But technological advancements do not necessarily lead to increased efficiency in narrative creation and development. For now, there seem to be more disadvantages to relying on automated journalism than there are advantages including increased possibilities of misinformation and disinformation. Aside from trepidation caused by the contraction of jobs in the media sector, there is also an anxious consternation about the credibility and quality of automated journalism and its use of algorithms.

AI is not ready to replace human rhetorical skills in storytelling such as humor, sarcasm, creativity, parody, and perhaps most importantly, critical thinking, even though these are all vital for proficient media professionalism. This has not stopped news editors from using AI and its algorithms to report weather conditions and corporate earnings. While this type of content creation is very advanced in comparison to conventional news-gathering methods, the adapted use of automated journalism to tell unique and human stories is still not as descriptive as conventional forms. Natural language processing and machine learning can have wide-ranging applications in building knowledge from internet-based news content. But this method has its drawbacks, as Gordon-Murnane (2018) discussed: "One of the most popular of AI techniques—machine learning—requires vast training datasets to identify and reveal hidden patterns in the data. However, many of these training sets can suffer from a variety of biases" (para. 1).

Despite the intention to be unbiased, automated journalism is only as non-biased as the program and algorithm upon which it is predicated. Even though news is reported with the aim of being impartial and objective, the output is still subject to implicit biases. The interpretations of the messaging derived from automated journalism are exacerbated by framing, which takes its cues from the original written narrative.

Newsrooms that have the means to create a more robust means of using AI and algorithms in their editorial development may have cogent ways of mitigating biases. However, there should be consideration about smaller newsrooms and nonprofit organizations that could use this technology to formulate specific narratives. The use of AI-powered tools, such as natural language processing and machine learning, is largely restricted to special stories and reports and is in many ways marginalized in news gathering. However, evolving forms of automated journalism will continue to have a substantive impact on publishing by mainstream news media outlets. While battling cases of "fake" content and news, the means of producing detailed and diversified information from verifiable sources is imperative. The *Financial Express* wrote that "automated journalism is also perceived as a threat to the authorship and quality of news and the precariousness of employment within the industry" (2019, 1).

One of the issues that news consumers face is the danger of an echo chamber where they receive news from a source that reflects what they are already thinking or that supports their intrinsic biases. By understanding the concept of agenda-setting theory, which indicates that media have the ability to influence the importance assigned to subject matter, the use of AI algorithms deriving inputs from the public agenda could have a strong influence on the narrative output by way of a set public agenda created by media sources. If this dynamic is not deterred but instead hyper-focused on the money-making aspects of the technology, this could augment biases occurring in duality from the reader and from the technology that is exacerbating the myopic understanding of newsworthy events. The implications for the detriment of the public good and democracy are elevated if diversity and proper stewardship of AI technologies are not monitored in a responsible way. This research suggests that AI and algorithmic journalism could have a deleterious impact on news comprehension, especially on marginalized groups that do not have the benefit of mainstream attention.

Bias is no more than the propensity to prejudge a mentally recorded piece of information as something that is favorable to a self-serving consumer. People engage in bias every day to make decisions. This happens when someone turns on the television and selectively watches channels; this is de facto bias, similar to algorithms selectively agglomerating information from sources that could exclude other viewpoints. A consumer who views this information would then engage in a fill-in-the-blank way to perceive the information based on the framing of the story. These interpretations can transform into implicit judgments that could lead to misinformed notions.

There is a need to examine issues surrounding AI use. The inchoate urgency is being focused on by numerous countries, governments, citizens, schools, and businesses. Discussions of whether there should be an AI-focused constitution, or another binding document, have yet to be fully convened. Nearly sixty countries have recommended a national strategy to encourage the responsible adoption of AI in various living and working spaces. In October 2022, the White House, under the Biden administration, created a "Blueprint for an AI Bill of Rights." The document, which also exists online, recommends ways to demystify AI results while directing the technology in a way that would be less discriminatory against certain groups but at the same time more discerning to ensure the safety of its users. While the White House mentions the need to pay attention in areas related to education, medicine, health care, finances, and security, it does not detail what policy will specifically address in our media institutions. Regardless, the lack of policy codification does not ensure responsible actions in implementing the technology's application, something that the US Congress has not considered in a fundamentally substantive way.

Media biases fueled by algorithmic assertion could adversely affect marginalized groups, including Black Americans as historically indicated. These biases can transform into discrimination as protected classes are ignored. People possess a level of trust in the media, which is motivated by sociocultural interaction. Society collectively assesses decisions that force evaluation of another person's veracity at the risk of creating harm. This relationship applies to media in a global marketplace. In a world where it is important to know how attitudes and beliefs about groups can support or degrade social understanding, the relationship reflects how decisions are made based on information. The use of algorithms in news media, especially with Knowhere, is most often to provide readers with unbiased information and challenge implicit bias. However, limiting the information could exacerbate an already problematic condition. It is important to note that biases have many forms; technology can be utilized to mitigate those biases. Overall, ethical AI ensures that the advancement of technology is involved with emulating human values beneficial to the human experience while underscoring the fundamental responsibilities that AI-powered activities are tasked with.

As the popularity of AI platforms increases, evident by the number of AI domain registration extensions (.AI), it is questionable whether AI algorithms will ever be perfectly neutral when distributing information, despite the intended objectives of platform architects. Bias in products derived by automated means will always reflect the inclinations of their creators. For this reason, it would make sense that the derivatives of algorithmic expression be interrogated deliberatively and unequivocally. Media communications are vital to the efficient operations of a democratic society. It is imperative that automated journalism endeavors supported by algorithms be examined for biases, whether accidentally performed or on purpose. It is only through this assiduous attention that we as a society create a happy, healthy, and productive AI-supported future.

Conclusion

Framing and thematic analyses assisted in identifying and examining the findings in the narratives of the studied publications and platforms. Through rigorous evaluative methods, various themes were extrapolated from the data. Framing analysis has been used to describe how people contextualize certain figures and events. Scholars who have used framing as a methodological framework have explicated it as a device used in politics, entertainment, and media (Zhongdang & Kosicki, 1993, 57). Thematic analysis has been used to analyze stories and narratives to understand patterns of understanding. Qualitative research can reveal information about the publications' content made through inferences. Both methods of analyses were important to understand media relationships related to automated media. A qualitative analysis found several themes associated with race and culture in the studied publications.

As Shanto Iyengar (1991) explained, stories that contain context, history, and background report news events as single episodes. He contended that episodic framing often reinforces the status quo, while thematic framing encourages change in society. This chapter reports the findings in sections. As Knowhere, the automated journalism media publication studied in this research, uses algorithms to find pre-eminent articles about a particular topic from leading online publications, it serves as the foundation for understanding differences between the emergent technology and conventional methods. Results are reported according to the research questions posed.

Publications for this study were aggregated from seven sources: three Blackcentric sources, three mainstream (white-owned) sources, and one automated (AI and algorithmically generated) source. Knowhere uses a system that selects news stories from the internet to agglomerate content using algorithms powered by a narrow form of AI. Data for this research included news stories written within the two-week period leading up to the 2018 midterm election day. More than 5,000 articles were screened for headlines and general article content. Articles that fit the criteria (*N*= 272), focusing on Black politicians and Blackcentric content, served as the necessary units of analysis.

The publications were assembled as a data set that was promoted in the Blackcentric, mainstream, or automated news sources related to the Black experience in America. Table 14.1 shows the tally of articles.

The time period leading up to the election included various newsworthy events that reached peak saliency in the zeitgeist, which included: the Georgia gubernatorial race, the Florida gubernatorial race, the Maryland gubernatorial race, voter suppression, a mail bomb scare, the appearance of blackface, and the lives of gubernatorial candidates Andrew Gillum, Stacey Abrams, and Ben Jealous.

OVERVIEW OF FINDINGS

Results stemming from the data analysis revealed four findings. First, emerging themes varied in topical nature, resulting in targeted coverage that highlighted Blackcentric content and issues relevant to the Black community or diminished the topical importance of content corresponding to Black society. Second, there was some consistency among the publications, as the narratives were closely concatenated to the chronology of the midterm political elections. Third, while there were some similarities among the publications, there were also distinct differences in the use of headlines with social inferences aligning closely between automated and mainstream content. Fourth, the major differences in the publications were observed as Blackcentric media reported individual candidates as empowering, inspirational, authoritative figures in their communities while expressing narratives derived from automated news content. These disparate observations were more connected to the white-owned/mainstream media, as these characteristic attributions were diminished. The data also show that the automated journalism source is not influenced by framing and interpretation of specific coverage.

The similarities between mainstream media and automated content were expected because of agenda setting's fundamental concept of how news influences the zeitgeist and the method by which AI algorithms cull content from online news stories.

Discussion

The purpose of this study was to show how Black candidates are framed by automated media that utilizes AI and algorithms and compares to conventional media methods to enhance comprehension of results. This study that focuses on journalism and progressive digital technologies was grounded in thematic and framing analysis. Analyses indicated that the media adopt specific frames to categorize the meaning of events, the motivations of people, and the contextualization of place to introduce meaning to the public. Despite Knowhere's objectives to create unbiased media, the results indicated a bias not by politicization but rather by exclusion.

The method in which a story is framed and thematically derived offers insights into what the publishers consider important. The algorithms are programmed to make judgments about importance without sentient analysis. One of the touted benefits of automated journalism is the ability to make decisions without emotional intelligence affecting discernment. However, this study indicates that, even in a journalism platform, algorithms have the potential to promote biases and foibles of humans without human judgment.

Frames give a perspective of content through the use of specific language, catch phrases, puns, headlines, and placement of articles. All of these items can have an influence on what is salient to the publication. The predominant items in the article can be published in stark contrast to the information that is not presented. This disparity can influence messaging based on what is written in an article and regarded as important versus what is considered inconsequential.

Previous studies incorporated framing analysis to inspect media coverage of Black people during specific times and places during elections. Using previous studies as a metric, evidence derived from the publications in this study indicated that Knowhere, which uses algorithms and AI to create its news, derives much of its content from the internet.

This could have positive effects on consistency in the mainstream news sources that most people read. However, this also shows a weakness in its delivery. Whereas many of the news narratives in automated content were reported with accuracy, some viewpoints and stories about the Black community were excluded. This omission is glaring. It is clear that the algorithm's preference provides customized choices, but those choices can exclude the voices of marginalized and disenfranchised groups.

Studies such as one by Perkins and Starosta (2001) examined how news media analyzed selection and story form to determine news values. Their methods differed from Knowhere's method of selection. They made fundamental observations that "news values may incorporate journalistic biases that then insinuate themselves into the final news story" (73). Considering that journalism can facilitate understanding of a person's position in a news cycle, Perkins and Starosta (2001) examined ways to explain how framing analysis takes place in a news story.

Previous research on Black people in politics has shown that resistance is often portrayed in mainstream press as deviant and undesirable behavior

(Leopold & Bell, 2017). Rioting, disruptive protesting, rallies, and similar events can be depicted in a way that could taint the public's perception of activists and the perceived oppressed (Twomey, 2001). The focus on this aspect of disruption is in contrast to discussion of policy or the reasons for the protests. Douglas McLeod (2007) noted the destructive effects of media's sustained paradigm of protection, which tends to confirm bias for the status quo interest, resulting in the detriment of the disenfranchised. McLeod (2007) indicated that media coverage that runs counter to the majority culture is neglected in favor of news coverage patterns that typify mainstream media coverage. If there is coverage of the disruptive culture by the mainstream, it is usually disparaging and damaging to objectives aimed at improving the current state of the communities that they represent.

The findings in this study were also consistent with analysis in other studies that examined various digital media. One study that highlighted this dynamic is "The Newsworthiness and Selection Bias in News About Murder: Comparative and Relative Effects of Novelty and Race and Gender Typifications on Newspaper Coverage of Homicide," which discussed reported news about murder synthesized by journalistic newsworthiness assessment based on traditional race and gender stereotyping (Lundman, 2003). Oliver (2003) discussed the criminalization of Black men based on inferences in newspaper narratives about the African American male experience. These expectations of social constructs derived from automated content were associated with Knowhere's claims that it mined various stories to provide an unbiased depiction of the focus of the news story. Analysis was used to examine themes in coverage. Some themes were closely related; others were less salient. Although this study would not be considered longitudinal as AI technology used in journalism is still considered to be cutting-edge and inchoately applied to technodeterminist potentiality, the density of political coverage within a set of impactful days leading to an election provided a comprehensive look at the actors and events associated with a political election.

Biases that are often found in storytelling are consistent in contemporary newsroom mass media culture (Leo, 2005). The news media's stated objective to have "balance" in news coverage can sometimes lead to a condition that still produces relative bias (Edwards & Cromwell, 2009). Edwards and Cromwell theorized that the myth within modern journalism is the result of objectivity and that the concept that a good publication or broadcast reporter just collects and reiterates the news for audience consumption is a falsehood. They stated that the idea of unbiased journalism is "devoid of reality" (3). While an event happens objectively, the recording of that event is done selectively through the lens of the recorder. Knowhere tries to mitigate this selectivity by drawing on numerous selections that were largely considered to be neutral in their narrative origins. But, as this research suggests, even this process has flaws if the original selections excluded sources of information that could represent an alternate narrative or perspective.

The results of this study suggest a need for a high set of standards that promote confidence and ensure a level of ethical considerations built into the technology in the journalism industry. Considerations about bias are just as important to protect the integrity of AI-algorithmically generated news as data privacy and security issues that direct innovation and engineering today. Data are the fuel behind such an ambitious algorithmic product. That is because the most substantive tools need information. This naturally inspires questions about how data are collected and used before being distributed to the public. One of the most challenging questions that journalists, scholars, and computer engineers must address is how to eliminate bias, both intentional and unintentional.

Focusing attention on the mitigation of biases would lead to consideration of those who are traditionally marginalized or excluded from digital space. By incorporating information that decreases biases which have the potential to exacerbate racial and demographic disparities, systems can be created to produce more evenly nuanced and intentionally balanced news narratives. However, programming systems with these considerations would require evaluation of a multitude of factors to determine appropriate objectives.

For now, humans must program the expert AI system and associated algorithms that shape societal and global perspectives when applied in textual format. This is part of the reason why developments in AI must apply mindful practices that moderate the various types of bias that can exist without consideration of discursive diversity. A computer can make millions of decisions in minutes, but it cannot be assumed that it will make contextual and more detrimental ethical decisions based on values compatible with the social construct in which it is used. If private enterprises are not evaluating the repercussions now, federal policies could be implemented to address technological deficits. In the fast-paced world of technological emergence, regulations are needed. Technological gatekeepers will need to be intuitive in valuing trust and ethical programming to encourage balance and diverse perspectives. It is imperative that, at the intersection of communications and technology, system architects pay close attention to these issues.

Previous studies have not examined the automated elements of narrow AI. This study contributes to the existing literature on media coverage of Black politicos and events.

In the future, there should be more studies examining the potential biases in journalism generated through algorithmic means, especially in the context of its influence that is growing in the communications industry. Studying Blackcentric media in comparison to white-dominated/mainstream media is important to examine perceptions of potential or existing journalistic disparities. By looking at all perspectives, a diversified and in-depth look at overall news perspectives can be achieved. A study that uses one aspect of culturally relevant journalism over another is devoid of the nuances for racially salient events. More studies should examine Black Americans' portrayals within AI supported media storytelling. Black candidates' objectives and how they are covered from the beginning of their political careers to the end would be an additional area of comparison just as other candidates are covered. Continued in-depth examinations to understand automated journalism biases would allow for better context of a particular environment instead of just presenting only hand-picked events.

Theoretical Implications

At the foundation of agenda-setting theory is the concept that mass media sets the agenda for what people care about. Two basic assumptions of agenda-setting are that (a) the media filter and shapes what is distributed to the public, and (b) the more attention the media gives a topic, the more important it is given importance by the public.

Although recent examination of agenda-setting theory has been inconclusive in understanding the relationship between public prominence of news coverage and the internet, this study provides insight into how AI algorithms are situated within the theory, bringing it into the twenty-first century. Anyone with internet access can locate news without the constraint of limited sources. Thus, it is harder to make a convincing argument that agenda setting is as impactful as it is perceived by some. This research suggests that in Knowhere's use of the AI algorithmic system, the relationship between the public news agenda and algorithmically automated output shares an expected relationship.

When the agenda setting theory was developed in the early 1970s, the understanding of societal events was contextualized through offerings by news media (Dearing & Rogers, 1996). Because of the augmentation of the internet, access to information provided by it continues to expand. This indicates that there will be a greater need for monitoring biases, misinformation, or disinformation through the online media. Knowing that news media have grown in presence in the public sphere, society can construct a wide range of opinions based on information retrieval. The various ways that people can access and interpret information suggest that this area needs deliberative consideration before adopting the technology consummately without intense evaluation. More research is needed to understand the relationship between the internet and the public regarding news and information in terms of the effects of agenda setting.

This study extends work by McCombs and Shaw in its connection to agenda setting and its overall concept. The prevailing media coverage receives a level of attention from the public that is sustained by a cycle of stories occupying headspace based on their preeminence in a news cycle. Automated journalism elevates and consequently augments this attention to another level by virtually recycling this existing awareness when it produces content derived from what is already receiving narrative prominence.

In response to research question 1, similar themes emerged from the data with similarities between the mainstream media and the automated content. The Knowhere algorithm is specifically designed for the public news agenda to have a direct impact on the content to process and be used in the editing process. The divergence from the Blackcentric content seems to support the notion that thematic relations are not as connected to these published sources. The algorithm works through collation and aggregation.

The response to research question 2 indicates consistency that is provided by agenda setting at the time the news content is rendered and then accounted for by the processing algorithms. There was some consistency among the examined stories, but there were divergences as well. The agenda setting process directed by mass media has been modified and will continue to be the case. From the 1968 Chapel Hill study, the agenda setting concept has become more specific and complicated. The strength of agenda setting influences has changed dramatically, based on certain conditions of the recipients of that information and the issue that is treated in the news coverage.

As McCombs and Shaw (1972) discussed how agenda setting forms "pictures within the mind," the influence of headlines should not be underestimated. Perusing a headline is the reader's initial opportunity to understand the presented topic and to contextualize it. In response to research question 3, connections could be inferred by the effectiveness of article placement and headline content.

In response to research question 4, the differences in themes among the publications indicated the presence of the first two levels of agenda setting. Here it was observed that not only is material presented to the reader; ways to think about the material are also presented. With a focus on attribute salience and the public's attribute agenda, the issues that are presented in the automated media accomplish the first level of agenda setting by presenting the initial story and the second level of the story includes the attribution given to the topic.

The potency regarding the influence of agenda setting varies dramatically, depending on contingent conditions of its receivers of the information and concomitant issues. As the world becomes a more global village and audiences learn more about the world to form "pictures in their heads" about issues, the power of the media to influence should not be underestimated. Editors and programmers should consider how new online communication forms affect the agenda-setting process, due to constant regenerating news cycles and concatenate systems applications that depend on their integrity to assemble content.

Framing analysis in this research included observations to examine how individual stories are introduced and whether there are noticeable comparisons among the types of media. The study informs ideas about disparities in framing regarding events that stem from Black American society. The patterns of framing revealed by the qualitative findings and the thematic inferences derived from them support framing within an automated context. The results could indicate the future of framing in a digital context, dependent on the data from which it is aggregated.

Conventional media studied within the two-week time frame of this study published more material with news about the candidates in a skewed fashion. Coverage often highlighted struggle and conflict more than what may have been perceived in actual reality or in a first-hand observation of these accounts. These differences can lead to confusion or misrepresentation. Based on these findings, skepticism based on misrepresentation is consistent with reports from Gandy and Li (2005), who found disparate reporting about Black Americans. The publications of the frames by Knowhere, initially crafted by the mainstream news media in connection with the public agenda and then aggregated by Knowhere's AI algorithms, support findings in previous studies about the depiction of Black Americans and events relevant to their society. Cherry-Randle (2013) argued that stories about racial inequality have been framed in terms of relative risk. Even though journalists try to bring understanding in stories involving African Americans, the image is of victims or losers by societal standards (Gandy & Li, 2005).

Considering that agenda setting suggests that news media orchestrate awareness of the public agenda by offering subject matter specific to what people should be thinking about according to media gatekeepers, McCombs and Shaw's theoretical framework is still very much alive in the twenty-first century. This research suggests that agenda-setting theory connects to the method by which AI and algorithms work to create news in the automated journalism examples used in this study. Expert systems and ANI that use data from the public agenda to create news narratives written for public consumption align not just with the seminal works of the 1960s but also with theorist Walter Lippmann's work in the 1920s.

LIMITATIONS

This study has some limitations. Other framing techniques could provide other forms of examination within other populations, time frames, and publications. These framing techniques could evaluate editorial cartoons, editorials, GIFs, or memes. Looking at the regions from which these publications were derived could offer unique framing perspectives. However, the current method was selected to understand dynamics related to Black candidates and racialized events that occurred during the 2018 election cycle.

Interpretations made through framing are often done with prejudice. Therefore, even if readers believe that certain frames or themes are not done with truthfulness, the unconscious mind still creates the frames. These biases in reporting happen in the minds of readers. To provide additional insight to the framing analysis, audience frames and interpretations should be analyzed. Because audiences are actively engaged in processing information introduced by the media, an analysis of audience perceptions should be conducted in future studies to understand whether audiences perceive different frames. This was not studied here because of the focus of this research on the presentation and potential representation of the frame rather than its interpretations. Tying the elements would have been time-consuming and laborious.

The time frame used in this study was specific but could be expanded in future studies. This study focused on two weeks of the most intensive news coverage surrounding midterm elections, which generated enough data to perform the study. However, a year's worth of material could provide deeper insights. Knowhere's inception was in 2015, so the material that the company generated did not always reflect the depth of established news narratives similar to those within conventional news sources.

One of the main questions that researchers may have about the disparities discovered in this research could focus on why the dynamics occurred as they did. To learn more about this would require examination of the programming of the algorithms, which could be done in a quantitative study and deeper understanding of computer programming. Because this study was qualitative, it is subjective and does not show causality, as this was not the purpose of the study. An examination using different quantitative methods could shed light on existing ostensible disparities. However, this study included an analysis with an established positionality when analyzing the data. Individual biases that include behaviors directed by instinct could lead to very detailed data, but could also defer to data that defaults to researcher subjectivity.

Recommendations for Future Research

Automated and algorithmically based journalism and its iterations are becoming more normalized in the media industry. Currently, the impact of this technology can be observed when trained journalists are tasked with investigating more nuanced news stories instead of initiating perfunctory narratives. The use of computers can then be deployed to publish other content that it's programmed to do while generating more content and expanding coverage to wider and diverse audiences. However, if left unmonitored, automated journalism use will constantly be interrogated in reference to its accountability. Computers and algorithms have no sentient code of ethics to follow like conventional human journalists do when trying to maintain objectivity, truth, and/or ethical responsibilities. Of course, a self-disclosed algorithmic procedural process would also be hard to discern. There would need to be a focused effort to ensure that AI is part of the ethical considerations that govern the methods of human journalists.

This study focused on seven media sources: three Blackcentric sources, three white-owned/mainstream sources, and one automated media source. Since there are various biases across media types, future research could consider a more comprehensive look at the publications that Knowhere uses to shape its narratives.

A researcher could look at other companies that use automated methods of journalism. Technologies that incorporate artificially intelligent models into myriad platforms are becoming more popular. There are already discussions as to how ChatGPT, one of the most popular generative pre-trained transformer chatbots, could revolutionize the way we receive and interpret our news. NewsGPT states that it is "the world's first news channel to be generated entirely by artificial intelligence" (NewMediaWire, 2023). The newly introduced platform promises to deliver unbiased, fact-based news to a global audience, much like Knowhere did when it was released. There could be a deeper understanding of how these systems work under the guidance or programming that incorporates different sets of parameters or categorization processes.

Other populations and their representations in media could also be further studied. There are members of marginalized groups such as within LGBTQIA+ communities and those who identify as transhuman with digitally integrated cybernetic aspirations. Of course, some populations may be easier to study than others, but many could benefit from understanding that segments of the population may be underrepresented in the use of a complex AI algorithm that is intended to offer a full, unbiased narrative of individuals and events.

Ethical and societal issues must be addressed soon in view of rising interests and cost efficiencies by news sources that use AI and algorithmically based technologies. This shift in usage and practice could drastically change and improve the mode of production in journalism in terms of efficiency, but only if monitored properly. High-speed connections and programs involving AI are being developed, manufactured, and implemented. The use of AI in news and journalism has the potential to change the industry in impactful ways. However, it is essential for news organizations to carefully consider the impact and ethical considerations when using these more advanced technologies to ensure that they are used responsibly and in a responsible way that benefits society. Media political economy involving AI should also be observed and studied because of the strong implications that automated technology could have on the means of journalistic production and societal impact.

For futurists and technology experts in the field of journalism, this is an exciting time. But for gatekeepers, social scientists, and researchers, it is also important to examine the benefits and disadvantages of the deployment of this technology. For the public to embrace this technology, people must have confidence in the information source providing the information.

Improved understanding of how people interact with AI and algorithms is essential, particularly when the possibility of objectivity and perfection is connected to the use of algorithms. If data sets used in journalism are predicated on what is already being discussed in the zeitgeist or trending, as several AI programs already do, it is contingent on a heterogeneous society in the United States to be clear about the need for diversity and transparency. Despite provocative debate over who is responsible for deficiencies in automated journalism: technology or humans, humans are still in control. Humans are needed to be the gatekeepers, as they historically have been in news and information management, for equitable narrative news development using technologies that engage AI algorithms. However, as opposed to the previous system of white-dominated decision-making spaces, diversity is essential for journalistic technological developments to be successful.

AI is already here. Certain considerations are necessary to understand the important societal issues related to transparency, bias, and the volumes of data that AI will process to be effective. People need to trust that AI is being utilized proficiently in all areas where the human mind would normally make decisions. There may need to be a set of standards that promote trust and confidence in the technology, just as security and data privacy are directing emerging programs of computer engineering. Governments across the world are starting to explore these complex issues regarding biases, information omission, and how the public interprets messaging from the information it receives from automated sources. The United States introduced a set of regulatory principles for AI at the annual Consumer Electronics Show in Las Vegas in 2020, where the improvement of deep fakes, the manipulation of video and audio, took center stage (Rahman, 2020). As AI implementation becomes more advanced, the Associated Press is taking a position that stresses responsible pragmatism by vetting materials carefully (Bauder, 2023).

The standards that would be expected in this area should be connected to comprehension of data that is essential to AI operations and processing. The supply of information drives machine learning, a necessary procedure in AI functionality. This information should be diverse, especially if it involves communications to an increasingly diverse population persuaded by individualized identity proclivities. This raises concerns about how diverse data and information are collected, utilized, disseminated, and protected. When considering information, it raises issues about the potential severity of digital hegemony on consumer populations.

One of the most challenging questions that researchers and academicians face is how to address biases, even if they are accidental. The call for institutions to include diverse people in their AI working spaces should be considered, especially as the technologies expand in journalism. Other suggestions allude that companies using this technology should only utilize it after specifically sourcing diverse materials to be modified and customized after human intervention. Offering more diverse information and data can create systems that produce news representing a larger section of the population and do not ignore or marginalize experiences of members of that population.

Although the autonomy of AI and its algorithmic expressions are appealing, a human programs the AI and algorithms, and that human's global views will mold the way that they, in effect, "teach" the technology, much like a child trying to understand its purpose and motivations based on instruction from a parent. Journalism is just one industry where businesses that are building AI systems must consider diversity in the workforce and install best strategies to mitigate accidental, inherent, or intentional biases.

Scholars and industry experts are widely in agreement when examining potential merits and dangers of the implementation of data-driven algorithmically generated news content. "Robot journalism" producers and disseminators must be held accountable for how they present news narratives to society. Humans will need to spot shortcomings in journalistic algorithmic computations in narratives to safeguard more integrity and conventional balance. AI and the algorithms that it uses are only as good as the patterns that engineers teach it. It will be necessary to follow the process from the beginning to the end. This suggests that scholarship regarding automated journalism is needed.

Diversity and transparency must also be a part of conversations about AI algorithms and their commercial applications. A complex computer system can output a complex computation and render a decision instantaneously, but would it be a correct and/or accurate decision when the modus operandi is without human intervention? Systems driven by AI and algorithms are supported by individuals with unique experiences, cultures, backgrounds, and biases, all of which, when developing programming, can influence unconsciously isolated experiences and introduce fundamental biases. This issue will be exacerbated by programmers or programming teams that may not represent the diversity in the greater society. This lack of programmed cultural diversification and information heterogeneity could lead to skewed datasets and algorithms that sustain systemic biases.

If the private sector is not addressing these concerns, the US government or influential lawmakers and policy makers will expectedly be forced to do so. With the increased pace of technological development in AI and its intersections of machine learning, natural language processing, and deep learning, regulations will most likely lag in a constant cycle to catch up. Technological (or techno) hegemony in the digital space is already being discussed in regard to the relationship between China and United States (Rikap et al., 2021). However, digital hegemony discussions are rarely mentioned pertaining to the intracontinental or domestic spaces. Congress will be strongly encouraged to take on these matters more seriously so as not to further alienate or misrepresent members of the public. Thus, it is imperative for companies and nonprofit organizations to lead the charge by adopting standards that encourage confidence and trust by providing a range of perspectives. It may even be necessary for workers to complete specific training standards when programming AI algorithms in news and journalism to minimize human prejudices from entering the system as much as can be avoided. It is important that people who work in the field have a substantive foundation on these very important issues about the future of communications.

With a dearth of attention focused on culturally Black American issues in news and public affairs commentary, it would be in the best interests of cultural understanding to address what could potentially be a lack of diversified voices overlooked by AI algorithms and the preclusion of information and data in increased automation. With news companies looking for ways to improve news-writing efficiency and augment reporter capability, it is important to include various voices from the public to represent a balanced view of who comprise the society that is being covered.

We are not yet close to duplicating how humans think and perform tasks, but we are steadily getting closer. Society is still a distance away from AI algorithms working in full autonomy to create news narratives. The scenario when a storytelling robot performs a rigorous newsgathering process on its own to eventually win a Pulitzer Prize is still a distance away. But AI and algorithms are making inroads into how publishers communicate and how the public retrieves information. This enhanced form of news gathering, which could be described as augmented digital news gathering or advanced digital news gathering (ADNG), has gigantic implications for how the public retrieves its information. AI, done correctly, could improve human culture in efficiency, speed, and output. However, development and installation of AI and algorithms into media institutions must be done mindfully to encourage a level of societal trust, inclusion, and improved accuracy.

There is a deficit of African American and Black presence in developing news narratives across the board, especially when factoring in media consolidation. The United States has experienced the shuttering of prominent

Blackcentric magazines and TV broadcasts. Radio stations are challenged (Disappearing Voices, 2009). Although spaces for Blackcentric voices have expanded over the internet contemporaneously with the shrinkage of conventional media, the wide dissemination of online hard news still faces disparities in equitable coverage based on editors' decisions. There should be some assurance that Black voices are included in important narratives, especially in the light of emergent technologies. Failure to monitor news narratives developed by artificial intelligence and algorithms could perpetuate the stifling of voices, the lack of diversity, and misunderstanding of those from marginalized communities.

Despite its potential, automated journalism and AI-supported storytelling, if left to its own automatic machinations without human evaluation and monitoring, could further exacerbate disparities without proper attention to a concept that could be defined as digital narrative neglect. Because of the omnipresence of media in their many iterations, from broadcast to online media to print media, they are in a position of influence over public awareness. As the *Financial Express* (Kabir, 2019) contended, "Automated journalism transforms structured data into news articles, and the quality of the output is highly dependent on the quality of the data that is fed into it." Acknowledging racial influence is important for encouraging ethical and responsible AI creation. We need to actively collaborate with stakeholders from myriad backgrounds, especially those who are disproportionately affected by biases that are integrated into AI and algorithm data sets. Humans are still detrimentally instrumental in ensuring that AI algorithms and the models derived from them are ethically created. Furthermore, the implementation of these technologies is also important and needs to be monitored to avoid racialized perpetuation and the normalization of biases.

Consequently, it is imperative that minority groups be included in the creation and delivery of content whether it is systemically or creatively. AI and algorithms as part of machine learning are growing. This growth will lead to challenges for members not within the status quo to be included in the narratives. Without proper stewardship, augmentation of this advanced method of news production will contribute to the disparate dominance of mainstream outlets and underrepresented narratives about Black society. Unique modes of digital or techno hegemony will increase exponentially within societies. Feelings of disenfranchisement could worsen, leaving many detached from the comforts of societal cohesion. Discrepancies regarding cyber equity should be observed and mitigated.

The necessity to acknowledge racial implications in AI biases is imperative to promote transparency, fairness, equality, equity, and the enhancement of the human user experience by developing ethical and responsible AI formation. AI and algorithms have the potential to enhance human experience and boost production. While AI systems can do many things well, it is still not AGI. Humans are an essential component in the decision-making process to understand where gaps and deficits in coverage can occur, leading to flawed information. By acknowledging these implications, we as a society can build future technological systems that strive to be more equitable, have diminished biases, and can better serve the needs of society. The evolution and diligent implementations of AI and associated algorithms in communications must be taken seriously and implemented deliberatively in the interests of accuracy to diverse perspectives and equitable representations.

Appendix A: Framing Categories

PUBLICATIONS

Mainstream

1. New York Times (NYT)
2. USA Today (USAT)
3. Washington Times (WASHT)

BLACKCENTRIC/BLACK AMERICAN

1. TheAfro.com
2. TheGrio.com
3. TheRoot.com

AUTOMATED

1. Knowhere

PUBLICATION UNIT OF ANALYSIS

1. Article
2. Editorial

CHARACTERIZATION OF INDIVIDUAL OR GROUP

1. Favorable
2. Unfavorable
3. Neutral

ARTICLE/EDITORIAL THEME

1. Champion of civil rights
2. Lionizing of the Underdog
3. Hero
4. African American fighter
5. Radical
6. Threat to democracy
7. White naivete
8. White oppression
9. Voter Suppression
10. Civil Rights Sustenance
11. Acts of Violence Against Black Politicians
12. Protests
13. Other

ARTICLE/EDITORIAL THEMATIC CONSISTENCY

1. Pro
2. Anti
3. Neutral
4. Article Placement (determined by the prospective length of each publication)

ARTICLE LENGTH—NUMBER OF WORDS IN EACH ARTICLE

1. 0–500
2. 501–1,000
3. 1001–1,500
4. 1501–2,000
5. 2,000+

HEADLINE DESCRIPTORS

1. Positive
2. Negative
3. Neutral

Appendix B: Audit Trail for Case Study

Ethics Training Certificate	Completed CITI-online training module with the RCR training on September 27, 2016.
Concept Paper Approval	The concept paper for this study was approved on October 7, 2018.
Pilot Study	A study was conducted between October and November 2018.
Dissertation Proposal	The dissertation proposal was approved on November 13, 2018.
Institutional Review Board	IRB approval was obtained for this study on March 28, 2019.
Literature Review	An initial literature review was developed as part of a research proposal and was approved in April of 2019.
Conceptual Framework	A constructivist approach was taken in this study, leading to thematic analysis and a qualitative framing method.
Participant Selection	Purposive sampling was used for selecting samples.
Data Collection and Storage	Additional data was created by this researcher, including an audit trail. This was combined with a researcher to create a reflective journal. This data was secured in a password-protected computer. All relevant and connected digital files were reinforced using a password-protected Google Drive account.
Coding Scheme	MaxQDA software was used to create and organize categories based on thematic network analysis. Basic themes, organizing themes, and narrative themes were developed through thematic network analysis. The coding framework included text segments based on qualitative thematic analysis.
Trustworthiness	Triangulation of data from alternate sources, member checking, reflective journaling, and a pilot study were all used in this study.

Reporting Findings   A thematic network analysis chart was used to display
                       themes taken from the coded data. These same themes
                       were used to answer the proposed research questions.

References

Aarøe, L. (2011). Investigating frame strength: The case of episodic and thematic frames. *Political communication, 28*(2), 207–226.

About USA today. (2018). Retrieved from https://marketing.usatoday.com/about

Adair, John (February 3, 2009). *The Art of Creative Thinking: How to be Innovative and Develop Great Ideas*. Kogan Page Publishers. ISBN 9780749460082.

Afro: The Black Media Authority. (2023). About Us. Afro.com. Retrieved from https://afro.com/about-us/

The Afro Staff. Ben Jealous for Governor. (2018). Retrieved from https://www.afro.com/ben-jealous-for-governor/

Ahn, G., Park, Y. J., & Hur, S. (2016). The dynamic enterprise network composition algorithm for efficient operation in cloud manufacturing. *Sustainability, 8*(12), 1239.

Akerkar, R. (2018). *Artificial Intelligence for Business*. Sogndal, Norway: Springer Nature Switzerland AG.

Akil II, B. (2007). *African American news websites: Publishers' views, perspectives and experiences in relation to the social construction of news, online news and the Black press*. The Florida State University.

Aladangady, A., & Forde, A. (2021). Wealth inequality and the racial wealth gap.

Alcorn, Jason. (2018). Knight Media Forum Focuses on Non-Profit News, Impact and Danger of Algorithms. *MediaShift*. Retrieved from http://mediashift.org/2018/02/no-doubts-impact-news-knight-media-forum/

Alford, N. (2018). Andrew Gillum Sends Message to Trump and DeSantis: The politics of hatred and separation have come to an end. *TheGrio.com*. Retrieved from https://thegrio.com/2018/11/06/andrew-gillum-sends-message-to-trump-and-desantis-the-politics-of-hatred-and-separation-have-come-to-an-end/

Alford, N. (2018). Can Stacey Abrams win over white voters in the South? This supporter says "yes." *TheGrio.com*. Retrieved from https://thegrio.com/2018/10/29/stacey-abrams-win-over-white-voters-in-the-south/

Alholjailan, M. I. (2012). Thematic analysis: A critical review of its process and evaluation. *West East Journal of Social Sciences, 1*(1), 39–47.

Allcott, H., & Gentzkow, M. (2017). Social media and fake news in the 2016 election. *Journal of Economic Perspectives, 31*(2), 211–36.

Allen, M. (2018). Published on Page 1 or 100? Editors & Publishers Discuss the Importance of Article Placement in a Magazine. Retrieved from https://www.free-lancewriting.com/magazine-writing/editors-discuss-article-placement/

Al-Salami, N. M. (2009). Evolutionary algorithm definition. *American J. of Engineering and Applied Sciences, 2*(4), 789–795.

Alterman, A. (1998, June). New media, new politics? Policy paper presented at the Washington Institute for Near East Policy, Washington DC.

Alvesson, M., & Deetz, S. (2000). *Doing critical management research*. London: Sage.

Anderson, Chris W. (2012). "Towards a Sociology of Computational and Algorithmic Journalism." *New Media and Society 7*(15): 1005–1021.

Antoine, L. (2014). Capital Press Club Celebrates 70th Anniversary, Honors Nine Media Legends. *Afro-American Red Star*, A.3.

Ardèvol-Abreu, A. (2015). Framing theory in communication research. Origins, development and current situation in Spain. *Revista Latina de Comunicación Social* (70).

Asante, M. (2011). *Afrocentric idea revised*. Temple University Press.

Associated Press. (2018). AI: automated insights. Retrieved from https://automate-dinsights.com/customer-stories/associated-press/

Associated Press. (2018, October 28). Police: Armed White Man Confronts Black GOP Volunteer. *Afro.com*. Retrieved from https://www.afro.com/police-armed-white-man-confronts-black-gop-volunteer/

Associated Press. (2018, November 1). Congressional Black Caucus chairman wants black in 1 of top 2 posts if Democrats take House. WashingtonTimes.com. Retrieved from https://www.washingtontimes.com/news/2018/nov/1/cedric-rich-mond-congressional-black-caucus-chairma/

Atlas. (2018). The 10 Most Popular Daily Newspapers in the United States. Retrieved from https://www.worldatlas.com/articles/the-10-most-popular-daily-newspapers-in-the-united-states.html

Auh, T. S. (1977). Issue Conflict and Mass Media Agenda-Setting during Bayh-Lugar Senatorial Campaign of 1974.

Bacchelli, A., & Bird, C. (2013, May). Expectations, outcomes, and challenges of modern code review. In Proceedings of the 2013 international conference on software engineering (p 712–721). IEEE Press. in *Education, 17*(2), 5–16.

Barnes, D. (1994). The Capital Press Club Continues To Be Needed. *Washington Informer*, 21.

Barrow, B. & Kinnard, M. (2018). Kamala Harris in South Carolina: "Fight for . . . who we are." *Afro.com*. Retrieved from https://afro.com/kamala-harris-in-south-carolina-fight-for-who-we-are/

Baskerville, R. L., & Wood-Harper, A. T. (2016). A critical perspective on action research as a method for information systems research. In *Enacting Research*

Methods in Information Systems: Volume 2 (p. 169–190). Springer International Publishing.

Bateson, G. (1972). *Steps to an ecology of mind: A revolutionary approach to man's understanding of himself.* New York: Ballantine Books.

Bau, V., Brough, M., Hartley, J., Hommel, E., Jiang, Y., Lie, R., Ling, R., Malikhao, P., Morley, D., Ogan, C. and Park, Y.J. (2014). *Technological determinism and social change: Communication in a tech-mad world,* 87–104. Lexington Books.

Bauder, D. (2023). AP, other news organizations develop standards for use of artificial intelligence in newsrooms. Retrieved from https://apnews.com/article/artificial-intelligence-guidelines-ap-news-532b417395df6a9e2aed57fd63ad416a

Baumgartner, F. R., & Jones, B. D. (April 18–21, 2001). Policy Dynamics. Annual Meeting of the Midwest Political Science Association. Chicago.

Bazeley, P. (2013). *Qualitative data analysis: Practical strategies.* Sage.

Bench-Capon, T. J., & Dunne, E. (2007). Argumentation in artificial intelligence. *Artificial intelligence, 171*(10–15), 619–641.

Benedict, L. (2014). *A critical synthesis and thematic analysis of the use of social media in higher education marketing* (Order No. 3635695). Available from ProQuest Dissertations & Theses Global. (1615348733). Retrieved from http://proxyhu.wrlc.org/login?url=https://search-proquest-com.proxyhu.wrlc.org/docview/1615348733?accountid=11490

Benton, M. & Frazier, P. J. (1976). The agenda-setting function of the mass media at three levels of "information holding." *Communication Research,* 3, 261–274.

Berkowitz, S. G. (1984). *Power and Hegemony: A South Italian Elite, 1800–1980 (Calabria, State, Class)* (Doctoral dissertation, University of Michigan).

Bialik, K. & Matsa, E. (2017). Key trends in social and digital news media. Retrieved from www.pewresearch.org/fact-tank/2017/10/04/key-trends-in-social-and-digital-news-media/

Bjornstrom, E. E. S., Kaufman, R. L., Peterson, R. D., & Slater, M. D. (2010). Race and ethnic representations of lawbreakers and victims in crime news: A national study of television coverage. *Social Problems, 57*(2), 269–293. Retrieved from doi:http://dx.doi.org.proxyhu.wrlc.org/10.1525/s2010.57.2.269

Boréus, K., & Bergström, G. (2017). Content analysis. Analyzing Text and Discourse: Eight Approaches for the Social Sciences, 23.

Bowen, G. A. (2009). Document analysis as a qualitative research method. *Qualitative Research Journal, 9*(2), 27–40. https://dx.doi.org/10.3316/QRJ0902027

Boyatzis, R. E. (1998). Transforming qualitative information: Thematic analysis and code development. Sage.

Boyd, A. (1994). *Broadcast Journalism, Techniques of Radio and TV News.* Oxford: Focal.

Boykoff, J. (2006). Framing dissent: Mass-media coverage of the global justice movement. *New Political Science, 28*(2), 201–228.

Brantner, C., Lobinger, K., & Wetzstein, I. (2011). Effects of visual framing on emotional responses and evaluations of news stories about the Gaza conflict 2009. *Journalism & Mass Communication Quarterly, 88*(3), 523–540.

Braun, V. & Clarke, V. (2006). Using thematic analysis in psychology. *Qualitative Research in Psychology, 3*, 77–101.

Brewer, P. R., & Gross, K. (2005). Values, framing, and citizens' thoughts about policy issues: Effects on content and quantity. *Political Psychology, 26*(6), 929–948.

Bridgewater, R. M., Smith, M. K., & Littlejohn, A. (2013). Influential News.

Brookshear, J. G. (2008). *Computer science: An overview.* Addison-Wesley Publishing Company.

Brosius, H. B. & Kepplinger, H. M. (1995). Killer and victim issues: Issue competition in the agenda-setting process of German television. *International Journal of Public Opinion Research, 7*(3), 211–231.

Brosius, H. B. Eps, (1995). Prototyping through key events. News selection in the case against aliens and asylum seekers in Germany. *European Journal of Communication 10*(3). 391–412.

Broussard, M. (2015). Artificial intelligence for investigative reporting: Using an expert system to enhance journalists' ability to discover original public affairs stories. *Digital Journalism, 3*(6), 814–831.

Brown, E. (2018). Undercover FBI agent provided "Hamilton" ticket for Andrew Gillum, Florida gubernatorial candidate, text messages say. *The Washington Times.* Retrieved from https://www.washingtonpost.com/investigations/undercover-fbi -agent-provided-hamilton-ticket-for-andrew-gillum-florida-gubernatorial-can-didate-text-messages-say/2018/10/23/ad21e0be-d6f3-11e8-83a2-d1c3da28d6b6 _story.html

Bucher, T. (2017). The algorithmic imaginary: Exploring the ordinary affects of Facebook algorithms. *Information, communication & society, 20*(1), 30–44.

Calhoun, C. J. (Ed.). (1992). *Habermas and the public sphere.* MIT press.

Caliendo, S. M., & McIlwain, C. D. (2006). Minority candidates, media framing, and racial cues in the 2004 election. *Harvard International Journal of Press/Politics, 11*(4), 45–69.

Campbell, J. L., Quincy, C., Osserman, J., & Pedersen, O. K. (2013). Coding in-depth semi-structured interviews: Problems of unitization and intercoder reliability and agreement. *Sociological Methods & Research, 42*(3), 294–320.

Carragee, K. M. (2019). Communication, activism and the news media: An agenda for future research.

Carlson, M. (2018). Automating judgment? Algorithmic judgment, news knowledge, and journalistic professionalism. *New Media & Society, 20*(5), 1755–1772. https://doi.org/10.1177/1461444817706684

Carlson, M. (2016). Automated journalism: A posthuman future for digital news? In *The Routledge companion to digital journalism studies* (p. 226–234). Routledge.

Carlson, M. (2015). The robotic reporter: *Automated journalism and the redefinition of labor, compositional forms, and journalistic authority. Digital Journalism, 3*(3):416–431.

Casey, D., & Murphy, K. (2009). Issues in using methodological triangulation in research. *Nurse Researcher, 16*(4), 40–55. https://doi.org/10.7748/nr2009.07.16.4 .40.c7160

Cassidy, W. (2016). Inching away from the toy department. *Communication & Sport*, *5*(5), 534–553. doi:10.1177/2167479516642205

Castellano, O. (2018). The Future of Journalism: Will Robots Get it Right? Retrieved from https://medium.com/@orge/this-is-the-future-of-journalism-will-a-machine -get-it-right-d3e747f16751

Chang , A., Levitt , M., Fox, K. (2022). The TV network Black News Channel goes off the air after 2 years. *NPR*. Retrieved from https://www.npr.org/2022/03/28 /1089311026/the-tv-network-black-news-channel-goes-off-the-air-after-2-years

Charles, G. U., & Fuentes-Rohwer, L. (2015). Habermas, the Public Sphere, and the Creation of a Racial Counterpublic. *Mich. J. Race & L.*, *21*, 1.

Chasmar, J. (2018, October 26). Democratic Sen. Joe Donnelly mocked for prais- ing minority staffers' work ethic. Washington Times.com Retrieved from https:// www.washingtontimes.com/news/2018/oct/31/joe-donnelly-dem-senator-mocked -praising-minority-/

Chéné, J. O., & Abad, G. L. (2014). The homogeneity process in the online media agenda. A comparative analysis of Spanish and foreign online Media/El proceso de homogeneización en la agenda cibermediática. análisis comparativo entre ciberme- dios españoles y extranjeros. *Comunicación y Sociedad*, *27*(3), 19–41. Retrieved from http://proxyhu.wrlc.org/login?url=https://search-proquest-com.proxyhu.wrlc .org/docview/1625907637?accountid=11490

Cherry-Randle, K. (2013). *Covering Conflict: How College Newspapers Framed Racial Incidents Involving African Americans, 1997–2009*. Scarborough: National Association of African American Studies. Retrieved from http://proxyhu.wrlc.org /login?url=https://search-proquest-com.proxyhu.wrlc.org/docview/1498460813 ?accountid=11490

Childs, J. (2011). The Black Press: Then and now. *The Louisiana Weekly*, 17.

Cho, J., & Trent, A. (2006). Validity in qualitative research revisited. *Qualitative research*, *6*(3), 319–340.

Choudery, H. (2018). Interview: Google AI Researcher Ilya Eckstein on what AI actually is and its impact on humanity. Retrieved from http://aimedianyone.org/all /podcast/interview-google-a-i-researcher-ilya-eckstein-on-what-a-i-actually-is-and -its-impact-on-humanity/

Chung, C. J., Kim, H., & Kim, J. H. (2010). An anatomy of the credibility of online newspapers. *Online Information Review*, *34*(5), 669–685. Retrieved from doi:http://dx.doi.org.proxyhu.wrlc.org/10.1108/14684521011084564

Chyi, H. I., & McCombs, M. (2004). Media salience and the process of framing: Coverage of the Columbine school shootings. *Journalism & Mass Communication Quarterly*, *81*(1), 22–35. doi:10.1177/107769900408100103

Clarke, V. & Braun, V. (2013). Teaching thematic analysis: Overcoming chal- lenges and developing strategies for effective learning. *The Psychologist*, *26*(2), 120–123.

Clerwall, C. (2014). Enter the robot journalist: Users' perceptions of automated con- tent. *Journalism Practice*, *8*(5), 519–531.

Cobb, R. W., & Elder, C. D. (1972). Participation in American politics: The dynamics of agenda-building. *(No Title)*.

Coddington, Mark. (2015). "Clarifying Journalism's Quantitative Turn: A Typology for Evaluating Data Journalism, Computational Journalism, and Computer-Assisted Reporting." *Digital Journalism, 3*(3): 331–348.

Cohen, B. C. (1963). *The press and foreign policy*. Princeton, NJ: Princeton University Press.

Cohen, L., Manion, L., & Morrison, K. (2011). *Research methods in education (7th ed.)*. New York, NY: Routledge.

Cohen, R., & Feigenbaum, E. A. (Eds.). (2014). *The handbook of artificial intelligence (Vol. 3)*. Butterworth-Heinemann.

Collective, B. S. (Ed.). (1995). *The black public sphere: A public culture book*. University of Chicago Press.

Constine, J. (2019). *Facebook changes algorithm to promote worthwhile & close friend content*. Retrieved from https://techcrunch.com/2019/05/16/facebook-algorithm-links/

Coombs, D. S., Lambert, C. A., Cassilo, D., & Humphries, Z. (2017). Kap takes a knee: A media framing analysis of Colin Kaepernick's anthem protest. In 20TH International Public Relations Research Conference (48). Retrieved from http://www.instituteforpr.org/wpcontent/uploads/IPRRC20-proceedings_Final.pdf#page=49.

Cotteleer, M. J., & Wan, X. (2016). Does the Starting Point Matter? The Literature-Driven and the Phenomenon-Driven Approaches of Using Corporate Archival Data in Academic Research. *Journal of Business Logistics, 37*(1), 26–33.

Cowart, H. S., Saunders, L. M., & Blackstone, G. E. (2016). Picture a protest: Analyzing media images tweeted from Ferguson. *Social Media+ Society, 2*(4), 2056305116674029.

Crawford, K. (2016). Artificial intelligence's white guy problem. *The New York Times, 25*.

Creswell, J. W. (2014) Research Design: Qualitative, Quantitative, and Mixed Methods Approaches. 4th Edition, SAGE Publications, Inc., London.

Creswell, J. W. (2013). *Research design: Qualitative, quantitative, and mixed methods approaches*. Sage publications.

Creswell, J. W. (2012). *Educational research: Planning, conducting, and evaluating quantitative and qualitative research (4 ed.)*. Boston, MA: Pearson Education, Limited.).

Creswell, J. W., & Poth, C. N. (2017). *Qualitative inquiry and research design: Choosing among five approaches*. Sage publications.

Crockett, S. (2018). Oprah Winfrey to Join Stacey Abrams on Her Historic Campaign to Become the First Black Woman Governor. TheRoot.com. Retrieved from https://www.theroot.com/oprah-winfrey-to-join-stacey-abrams-on-her-historic-cam-1830131124

Crunchbase. (2019). Knowhere: Overview. Retrieved from https://www.crunchbase.com/organization/knowherehq#section-related-hubs

Cummings, S., Bridgman, T., & Brown, K. G. (2016). Unfreezing change as three steps: Rethinking Kurt Lewin's legacy for change management. *Human Relations, 69*(1), 33–60.

Cummings, T. G., Worley, C. G. (2015). *Organization Development & Change (10th)*. Stamford, CT: Cengage Learning.

Cummings, W. (2018). Oprah Winfrey, Georgia governor hopeful Stacey Abrams targeted in racist robocall. USAToday.com. Retrieved from https://www.usatoday.com/story/news/politics/elections/2018/11/04/midterm-elections-2018-stacey-abrams-targeted-racist-robocall/1885908002/

Dartnall, T. (Ed.). (2013). *Artificial intelligence and creativity: An interdisciplinary approach (Vol. 17)*. Springer Science & Business Media.

Dawson, M. C., & Collective, B. S. (1995). The Black Public Sphere.

De Vreese, C. H. (2005). News framing: Theory and typology. *Information design journal+ document design, 13*(1), 51–62.

Dearing, J. W., & Rogers, E. (1996). *Agenda-setting* (Vol. 6). Sage publications.

Dearing, J. W., & Rogers, E. M. (1996). *Communication concepts 6: Agenda-setting*. SAGE Publications, Inc. California. ISBN 0-7619-0562-6 (c)

DeJarnette, Ben. (2016). 4 Examples of AI's Rise in Journalism (And What it Means for Journalists). Retrieved from mediashift.org/2016/09/4-examples-ais-rise-journalism-means-journalists/

Denscombe, M. (2014). *The good research guide: For small-scale social research projects*. McGraw-Hill Education (UK).

Denzin, N. K., & Lincoln, Y. S. (2011). *The Sage handbook of qualitative research*. Sage Publications Ltd.

Deuze, M. (2008). Journalism education in an era of globalization. In M. Löffelholz & D. Weaver (Eds.), *Global journalism research: Theories, methods, findings, future,* (p. 267–281). Malden, MA: Blackwell Publishing.

Devlin, E. K. (2023). Gettysburg 1963: Civil Rights, Cold War Politics, and Historical Memory in America's Most Famous Small Town by Jill Ogline Titus. *The Journal of the Civil War Era, 13*(2), 274–276.

Disappearing Voices—The Decline of Black Radio. (September 25, 2009). Benton Institute for Broadband & Society. Retrieved from https://www.benton.org/event/disappearing-voices—-decline-black-radio

Dixon, T. L. (2017). Good Guys Are Still Always in White? Positive Change and Continued Misrepresentation of Race and Crime on Local Television News. *Communication Research, 44*(6), 775–792. https://doi.org/10.1177/0093650215579223

Dixon, T. L., & Linz, D. (2000). Overrepresentation and underrepresentation of African Americans and Latinos as lawbreakers on television news. *Journal of communication, 50*(2), 131–154.

Dörr, K. N. (2016). Mapping the field of Algorithmic Journalism. Digital Journalism, 4(6), 700–722. https://doi.org/10.1080/21670811.2015.1096748

Druckman, J. N. (2001). The implications of framing effects for citizen competence. *Political behavior, 23*(3), 225–256.

Eargle, L. A., Esmail, A. M., & Sullivan, J. M. (2008). Voting the issues or voting the demographics? The media's construction of political candidates credibility. *Race, Gender & Class, 15*(3), 8–21, 23–25, 28–31. Retrieved from http://proxyhu.wrlc.org/login?url=https://search-proquest-com.proxyhu.wrlc.org/docview/218859354?accountid=11490

Eaton Jr, H. (1989). Agenda-setting with bi-weekly data on content of three national media. *Journalism Quarterly, 66*(4), 942–959.

Edsall, T. (2019). The Deepening 'Racialization' of American Politics: Obama was a lightning rod. Trump is a lightning strike. The New York Times. Retrieved from https://www.nytimes.com/2019/02/27/opinion/trump-obama-race.html

Edwards, D., & Cromwell, D. (2009). *Newspeak in the 21st Century.* London: Pluto Press.

Elber, L. and Kennedy, M. (2018). NBC Cancels Megyn Kelly's Show After Blackface Controversy. *Afro.com.* Retrieved from https://afro.com/nbc-cancels-megyn-kellys-show-after-blackface-controversy/

Elkrief, A. (2019, July 3). Phone interview with [A. Elkrief].

Elkrief, A. [Inverse]. (2019, July 19). *Inside Knowhere: News Written by Artificial Intelligence | Inverse* [video file]. Retrieved from: https://www.youtube.com/watch?v=ikzMTKRiN00

Elo, S., Kääriäinen, M., Kanste, O., Pölkki, T., Utriainen, K., & Kyngäs, H. (2014). Qualitative content analysis: a focus on trustworthiness. *Sage Open, 4*(1), 2158244014522633

Entman, R. M. (1993). Framing: Toward clarification of a fractured paradigm. *Journal of communication, 43*(4), 51–58.

Entman, R. M. (1991). Framing US Coverage of International. *Journal of communication, 41,* 4.

Entman, R. M., & Gross, K. A. (2008). Race to judgment: Stereotyping media and criminal defendants. *Law and Contemporary Problems, 71*(4), 93–133.

Ernst, D. (2018). Dem candidate caught taking Republican opponent's campaign material. *Washington Times.* Retrieved from https://m.washingtontimes.com/news/2018/oct/23/monique-johns-dem-candidate-caught-taking-republic/

Etikan, I., Musa, S. A., & Alkassim, R. S. (2016). Comparison of convenience sampling and purposive sampling. *American Journal of Theoretical and Applied Statistics, 5*(1), 1–4.

Eubanks, V. (2018). *Automating inequality: How high-tech tools profile, police, and punish the poor.* St. Martin's Press.

Fairhurst, G., & Sarr, R. (1996). *The art of framing.* San Francisco: Jossey-Bass.

Fandos, N. (2018). A Black Senate Candidate Stumps in Mississippi, but His Party Holds Him Back. *The New York Times.* Retrieved from https://www.nytimes.com/2018/10/25/us/politics/mike-espy-mississippi-black-senator.html

Fanta, Alexander. (2018). Robots can save local journalism, but will they make it more biased? With local journalism on the decline, robots are here to stay. Retrieved from: https://datajournalism.com/read/longreads/robots-can-save-local-journalism-but-will-they-make-it-more-biased

Farber, M. (2017). The future of journalistic labor in the age of digital narratives: the algorithmic authority or automated news as a legitimate knowledge producer. *Psychosociological Issues in Human Resource Management, 5*(2), 199–204. Retrieved from doi:http://dx.doi.org.proxyhu.wrlc.org/10.22381/PIHRM52201710

Fausset, R. (2018). After a Primary on the Fringe, Georgia Republican Tacks Toward the Center. *The New York Times*. Retrieved from https://www.nytimes.com/2018/09/02/us/politics/kemp-georgia-abrams.html

Feldman, S. (2019). Newspaper Industry: Then & Now Newspaper Circulation. Statista. Retrieved from https://www.statista.com/chart/18827/united-states-newspaper-circulation/

Fields, M. (1944). The Negro Press and the Issues of Democracy. *From address delivered before the First Annual Dinner of the Capital Press Club in Washington, DC*.

Fine, T. S. (1992). The impact of issue framing on public opinion: Toward affirmative action programs. *The Social Science Journal, 29*(3), 323–334.

Flippin-Wynn, M. (2010). *Causing a ruckus: Racial framing in political blogs during the 2008 presidential campaign*. Retrieved from http://proxyhu.wrlc.org/login?url=https://search-proquest-com.proxyhu.wrlc.org/docview/610187763?accountid=11490

Frazier, S. (1972). *The Utopian Vision Of The Movement, 1968–1970: A Thematic Analysis Of Selected Underground Newspapers* (Order No. 1304407). Available from ProQuest Dissertations & Theses Global. (302665084). Retrieved from http://proxyhu.wrlc.org/login?url=https://search-proquest-com.proxyhu.wrlc.org/docview/302665084?accountid=11490

Fredrickson, G. M. (1996). *Black Liberation: A comparative history of Black ideologies in the United States and South Africa*. Oxford University Press.

Fridkin, Kim, et al. (2017). Race and Police Brutality: The Importance of Media Framing. *International Journal of Communication (11)*, p. 3394–3414.

Friedman, A. (1979). Framing pictures: The role of knowledge in automatized encoding and memory for gist. Journal of Experimental Psychology: General, 108, 316–355.

Friedman, B., & Nissenbaum, H. (1996). Bias in computer systems. *ACM Transactions on information systems (TOIS), 14*(3), 330–347.

Fritz, S., & Foreword By Brooks, R. (2002). *Understanding artificial intelligence*. Warner Books, Inc.

Funder, D. C., Levine, J. M., Mackie, D. M., Morf, C. C., Sansone, C., Vazire, S., & West, S. G. (2014). Improving the dependability of research in personality and social psychology: Recommendations for research and educational practice. *Personality and Social Psychology Review, 18*(1), 3–12.

Funkhouser, R. (1973). The issues of the Sixties: An exploratory study in the dynamics of public opinion. *The Public Opinion Quarterly, 37*(1), 62–75.

Gamson, W. A. (1989). News as framing: Comments on Graber. *American Behavioral Scientist, 33*(2), 157–161.

Gamson, W. A., & Modigliani, A. (1989). Media discourse and public opinion on nuclear power: A constructionist approach. *American journal of sociology, 95*(1), 1–37.

Gamson, W. A. (1985). Goffman's legacy to political sociology. *Theory and Society*, 14, 605–621.

Gandy Jr., O. H., & Li, Z. (2005). Framing comparative risk: A preliminary analysis. *The Howard Journal of Communications, 16*(2), 71–86.

Gans, H. J. (1979). Symbolic ethnicity: The future of ethnic groups and cultures in America. *Ethnic and racial studies*, *2*(1), 1–20.

Garcia, D. L. (1996). Global Communications: Opportunities for Trade and Aid. *SAIS Review*, *16*(1), 35–66.

Gass, S., Mackey, A., & Ross-Feldman, L. (2005). Task-based interactions in classroom and laboratory settings. *Language learning*, *55*(4), 575–611.

Gerbner, G., & Gross, L. (1976). Living with television: The violence profile. *Journal of communication*, *26*(2), 172–199.

Gerhards, J., & Rucht, D. (1992). Mobilization: Organizing and framing in two protest Campaigns in West Germany. *American Journal of Sociology*, 98, 555–595.

Gesenhues, A. (2017). Pew Research Center says 45% of Americans get their news from Facebook. The number of people getting news from social media continues to increase. Third Door Media, Inc. Retrieved from https://martech.org/pew-research -center-says-45-americans-get-news-facebook/

Ghanem, S. (2002). Filling in the tapestry: The second level of agenda-setting. In M. McCombs, D. Shaw & D. Weaver (Eds.) *Communication and democracy exploring the intellectual frontiers in agenda-setting theory* (p. 25–37). Mahwah, NJ: Lawrence Erlbaum Associates.

Ghanem, S. I. (1996). *Media coverage of crime and public opinion: An exploration of the second level of agenda-setting*. The University of Texas at Austin.

Ghanem, S. & D. Evatt (1995, August). The paradox of public concern about crime: An interim report. Paper presented at the annual meeting of the Association for Education in Journalism and Mass Communication, Washington, D.C.

Gibson, A. J., Lewando-Hundt, G., & Blaxter, L. (2014). Weak and strong publics: Drawing on Nancy Fraser to explore parental participation in neonatal networks. *Health Expectations*, *17*(1), 104–115.

Gläser, J., & Laudel, G. (2013, March). Life with and without coding: Two methods for early-stage data analysis in qualitative research aiming at causal explanations. In *Forum Qualitative Sozialforschung/Forum: Qualitative Social Research* (Vol. 14, No. 2).

Goffman, E. (1974). *Frame analysis: An essay on the organization of experience.* Harvard University Press.

Golafshani, N. (2003). Understanding reliability and validity in qualitative research. *The Qualitative Report*, *8*(4), 597–606.

Golan, G., & Wanta, W. (2001). Second-level agenda-setting in the New Hampshire primary: A comparison of coverage in three newspapers and public perceptions of candidates. *Journalism and Mass Communication Quarterly, 78*(2), 247–259. Retrieved from http://proxyhu.wrlc.org/login?url=https://search-proquest-com .proxyhu.wrlc.org/docview/216929826?accountid=11490

Goldberg, E., Driedger, N., & Kittredge, R. I. (1994). Using natural-language processing to produce weather forecasts. *IEEE Expert*, *9*(2), 45–53.

Gonzenbach, W. J. (1992). A time-series analysis of the drug issue, 1985–1990: The press, the president and public opinion. *International Journal of Public Opinion Research 4*(2), 126–147.

Gordon-Murnane, L. (2018). Ethical, explainable artificial intelligence: Bias and principles. *Online Searcher, 42*(2), 22–24, 40–44. Retrieved from http://proxyhu .wrlc.org/login?url=https://search-proquest-com.proxyhu.wrlc.org/docview /2272763960?accountid=11490

Gottfried, J., & Shearer, E. (2017). Americans' online news use is closing in on TV news use. *Pew Research Center, 7.*

Graefe, A. (2017). The Conversation: How algorithms and human journalists will need to work together. Retrieved from https://theconversation.com/how-algorithms -and-human-journalists-will-need-to-work-together-81869

Graefe, A. (2016). Guide to Automated Journalism. (2016). Retrieved from file:///C: /Users/kidha/Downloads/GuideToAJ%20(1).pdf

Gray, J. H., Reardon, E., & Kotler, J. A. (2017, June). Designing for Parasocial Relationships and Learning: Linear Video, Interactive Media, and Artificial Intelligence. In Proceedings of the 2017 Conference on Interaction Design and Children (p. 227–237). ACM.

Green, M. (2018). Black Women Save Politics. *Afro.com.* Retrieved from https://afro .com/black-women-save-politics/

Grieco, E. (2018). Newsroom employment dropped nearly a quarter in less than 10 years, with greatest decline at newspapers. Retrieved from http://www.pewre-search.org/fact-tank/2018/07/30/newsroom-employment-dropped-nearly-a-quarter -in-less-than-10-years-with-greatest-decline-at-newspapers/

Gross, K. (2008). Framing persuasive appeals: Episodic and thematic framing, emotional response, and policy opinion. *Political Psychology, 29*(2), 169–192.

Grynbaum, M. M. (2017). Trump Strategist Stephen Bannon Says Media Should "Keep Its Mouth Shut." *New York Times, 26.*

Habermas, J., & Habermas, J. (1991). The structural transformation of the public sphere: An inquiry into a category of bourgeois society. MIT press.

Hackforth, R. (Ed.). (1972). *Plato: Phaedrus* (No. 119). Cambridge University Press.

Hall, J. (2001). *Online journalism: A critical primer.* Pluto Press.

Haner, J., & Garcia, D. (2019). The artificial intelligence arms race: Trends and world leaders in autonomous weapons development. *Global Policy, 10*(3), 331–337.

Hansen, M., Roca-Sales, M., Keegan, J. M., & King, G. (2017). Artificial Intelligence: Practice and Implications for Journalism.

Harriot, M. (November 1, 2018). White Woman Calls the Cops on Black Woman for Canvassing In Wealthy Neighborhood. TheRoot.com. Retrieved by https:// www.theroot.com/white-woman-calls-the-cops-on-black-woman-for-canvassin -1830157131

Harriot, M. (October, 24, 2018). Black Voters in Georgia Say Something Funny Is Going on With Their Voting Machines. TheRoot.com. Retrieved from https:// www.theroot.com/black-voters-in-georgia-say-something-funny-is-going-on -1829979736

Harris, H. (2018). Jealous Running Hard in Final Days of the Campaign, Even as Polls Point to Hogan. *Afro.com.* Retrieved by https://afro.com/jealous-running -hard-in-final-days-of-the-campaign-even-as-polls-point-to-hogan/

Hart, R. (2000). *DICTION 5.0: The text-analysis program.* Thousand Oaks, CA: Sage.

Hashem, I. A. T., Yaqoob, I., Anuar, N. B., Mokhtar, S., Gani, A., & Ullah Khan, S. (2015). The rise of "big data" on cloud computing: Review and open research issues. Information Systems, 47, 98–115. https://doi.org/10.1016/j.is.2014.07.006

He, H., & Brown, A. D. (2013). Organizational identity and organizational identification: A review of the literature and suggestions for future research. *Group & Organization Management, 38*(1), 3–35.

Helms, J. E. (1994). The conceptualization of racial identity and other "racial" constructs. In E. J. Trickett, R. G. Watts, & D. Birman (Eds.). *Human diversity: Perspectives of people in context*, (p. 285–311). San Francisco: Jossey-Bass.

Helms, J. E., & Talleyrand, R. M. (1997). Race is not ethnicity. *American Psychologist*, 52, 1246–1247.

Hendrickson, L. (1995, May). Effects of framing uniformity on the perception of child neglect as a "family problem." Paper presented at the Mass Communication Division, Annual Conference of the International Communication Association, Albuquerque, NM.

Hennart, J. F., & Slangen, A. H. (2015). Yes, we really do need more entry mode studies! A commentary on Shaver. *Journal of International Business Studies, 46*(1), 114–122.

Henry wallace taking crusade into deep south. (1947, Nov 22). *The Pittsburgh Courier (1911–1950)* Retrieved from http://proxyhu.wrlc.org/login?url=https://search-proquest-com.proxyhu.wrlc.org/docview/202204484?accountid=11490

Hertog, J. K., & McLeod, D. M. (2001). A multiperspectival approach to framing analysis: A field guide. In *Framing public life* (p. 157–178). Routledge.

Hertog, J. K., & McLeod, D. M. (1995). Anarchists wreak havoc in downtown Minneapolis: A multi-level study of media coverage of radical protest. *Journalism & Mass Communication Monographs*, (151), 1.

Hobson, J. (2008). Digital Whiteness, Primitive Blackness. Feminist Media Studies, 8(2), 111–126. https://doi.org/10.1080/00220380801980467

Holody, K. J., Park, S. Y., & Zhang, X. (2013). Racialization of the Virginia Tech shootings: A comparison of local and national newspapers. *Journalism Studies, 14*(4), 568-583.

Holt, L. F., & Major, L. H. (2010). Frame and blame: An analysis of how national and local newspapers framed the Jena Six controversy. *Journalism & Mass Communication Quarterly, 87*(3–4), 582–597.

Houghton, C., Casey, D., Shaw, D., & Murphy, K. (2013). Rigor in qualitative case-study research. *Nurse Researcher, 20*(4), 12–17. https://dx.doi.org/10.7748/nr2013.03.20.4.12.e326

Howard, N. (2018). 11 News Sites We Love For Trail Blazing Coverage of Black Culture and Communities. Retrieved from https://mediablog.prnewswire.com/2018/02/14/top-african-american-news-sites/

Hrach, T. J. (2016). *The riot report and the news: How the Kerner Commission changed media coverage of Black America.* University of Massachusetts Press.

Ionescu, L., Lăzăroiu, G., and Şerban, S. (2013). A Theory of the Availability and Level of Consumer Protection in Online and Mobile Payments for Public Economic Services, *Amfiteatru Economic, 15*(34): 369–384

Ismail, K. (2018). AI vs. Algorithms: What's the Difference? *CMSWiRE.com.* Retrieved from https://www.cmswire.com/information-management/ai-vs-algorithms-whats-the-difference/

Iyengar, S. (1994). *Is anyone responsible?: How television frames political issues.* University of Chicago Press.

Iyengar, S. (1991). Is Anyone Responsible? Chicago, IL: University of Chicago Press.

Iyengar, S., & Simon, A. (1993). News coverage of the Gulf crisis and public opinion: A study of agenda-setting, priming, and framing. *Communication research, 20*(3), 365–383.

Jerome, C., Hie, T. S., Hadzmy, A. J. A., & Raslie, H. (2023). Do You Still Watch the News on TV? Examining TV News Viewing among Malaysians Today. *International Journal of Business and Technology Management, 5*(2), 85–93.

Johnson Jr., F. W. (1993). A history of the development of Black radio networks in the United States. *Journal of Radio Studies, 2*(1), 173–187.

Johnson, J. (October, 24, 2018). The Governor's Debate Between Stacey Abrams and Brian Kemp Is Everything That's Wrong with Georgia Politics. *TheRoot.com.* Retrieved from https://www.theroot.com/the-governor-s-debate-between-stacey-abrams-and-brian-k-1829957299

Kabir, Z. (2019). Technological advancements in present-day journalism: Prospects and challenges. *The Financial Express.* Retrieved from https://thefinancialexpress.com.bd/views/views/technological-advancements-in-present-day-journalism-prospects-and-challenges-1562943941

Kai, M. (2018). This Is Scary: Megyn Kelly Says "Blackface Was OK" for Halloween in Her Childhood [Updated]. TheRoot.com. Retrieved from https://thegrapevine.theroot.com/this-is-scary-megyn-kelly-says-blackface-was-ok-for-ha-1829941736

Kaid, L. L., & Wadsworth, A. J. (1989). Content analysis. *Measurement of communication behavior,* 197–217.

Kardaş, T. (2017). Trump and the rise of the media-industrial complex in American politics. *Insight Turkey, 19*(3), 93–120. Retrieved from doi:http://dx.doi.org.proxyhu.wrlc.org/10.25253/99.2017193.08

Kawamoto, K. (Ed.). (2003). *Digital journalism: Emerging media and the changing horizons of journalism.* Rowman & Littlefield Publishers.

Kee, Tameka. (June 10, 2009). "Can NBCU's TheGrio.com Succeed Where RushmoreDrive.com Failed?" CBS News. Retrieved March 27, 2013.

Kern, M. (2001). Disadvantage Al Gore in election 2000: Coverage of issues and candidate attributes, including the candidate as campaigner, on newspaper and television news web sites. *The American Behavioral Scientist, 44*(12), 2125–2139. Retrieved from http://proxyhu.wrlc.org/login?url=https://search-proquest-com.proxyhu.wrlc.org/docview/214768268?accountid=11490

Keyton, J. (2006). *Communication Research: Asking questions, finding answers.* London: McGraw-Hill Higher Education.

Kian, Edward T. M., Michael Mondello, and John Vincent. "ESPN—The Women's Sports Network? A Content Analysis of Internet Coverage of March Madness." *Journal of Broadcasting & Electronic Media*, vol. 53, no. 3, 2009, p. 477–495.

Kim, D., & Kim, S. (2017). Newspaper companies' determinants in adopting robot journalism. *Technological Forecasting and Social Change, 117*, 184–195.

Kim, H. S., & Cho, S. B. (2000). Application of interactive genetic algorithm to fashion design. *Engineering applications of artificial intelligence, 13*(6), 635–644.

Kim, S., Scheufele, D., & Shanahan, J. (2005). Who cares about the issues? Issue voting and the role of news media during the 2000 US presidential election. *Journal of Communication, 55*(1), 103–121.

Kim, S. H., Scheufele, D. A., & Shanahan, J. (2002). Think about it this way: Attribute agenda-setting function of the press and the public's evaluation of a local issue. *Journalism & Mass Communication Quarterly, 79*(1), 7–25.

King, E. G. (1990). Thematic coverage of the 1988 presidential primaries: A comparison of *USA Today* and the *New York Times. Journalism Quarterly, 67*(1), 83–87.

Kiousis, S. (2004). Explicating media salience: A factor analysis of *New York Times* issue coverage during the 2000 U.S. presidential election. *Journal of Communication*, 71–87.

Klein, A. G., Byerly, C. M., & McEachern, T. M. (2009). Counterframing public dissent: An analysis of antiwar coverage in the U.S. media. *Critical Studies in Media Communication, 26*(4), 331–350.

Knight, F. (2018). Georgia election fight shows that black voter suppression, a southern tradition, still flourishes. *Afro.com*. Retrieved from https://www.pbs .org/newshour/politics/georgia-election-fight-shows-that-black-voter-suppression -a-southern-tradition-still-flourishes

Knowhere, Inc. (2018). Retrieved from https://knowherenews.com/

Knowhere. (2018, October 29). Jimmy Carter calls for Brian Kemp to resign. Knowhere. Retrieved from https://knowherenews.com/event/366b9a09-9443-41fc -97c2-219458f59ed7?stance=0

KnowhereNews.com. (2019). KnowhereNews.com: About. Retrieved from https:// knowherenews.com

Koblin, J., & Grynbaum, M. M. (2018). Megyn Kelly's "Blackface" Remarks Leave Her Future at NBC in Doubt. *New York Times*.

Konradsen, H., Kirkevold, M., & Olson, K. (2013). Recognizability: A strategy for assessing external validity and for facilitating knowledge transfer in qualitative research. *Advances in Nursing Science, 36*(2), E66–E76.

Kusuma, M. (2014). Does culture tame the bunny? A content analysis of a global adult magazine. *Qualitative Market Research: An International Journal, 17*(1), 4–23.

Langham, T. (2017). 10 News Sites We Love for In-Depth Coverage of Black Culture & Communities. Retrieved from https://mediablog.prnewswire.com/2017/02/23/ african-american-news-sites/

Langmia, K. (2016). *Globalization and Cyberculture: An Afrocentric Perspective*. Springer.

Latar, N. L. (2018). Robot journalism. *Robot Journalism: Can Human Journalism Survive?*, 29.

Latar, N. L. (2015). The robot journalist in the age of social physics: The end of human journalism? In *The new world of transitioned media* (p. 65–80). Springer, Cham.

Lazarsfeld, P. F., & Merton, R. K. (1948). Mass communication, popular taste and organized social action. *Media studies*, 18–30.

Lazer, D. M., Baum, M. A., Benkler, Y., Berinsky, A. J., Greenhill, K. M., Menczer, F., . . . & Schudson, M. (2018). The science of fake news. *Science*, *359*(6380), 1094–1096.

Lee, A. M., Lewis, S. C., & Powers, M. (2014). Audience clicks and news placement: A study of time-lagged influence in online journalism. *Communication Research*, *41*(4), 505–530.

Lee, G. (2005). Agenda-setting effects in the digital age: Uses and effects of online media. Unpublished doctoral dissertation, University of Texas, Austin.

Lee, J. H., & Choi, Y. J. (2009). News values of sports events: An application of a newsworthiness model on the World Cup coverage of US and Korean media.

Lee, T., Ryan, W., Wanta, W. & Chang, K. (2004). Looking presidential: A comparison of newspaper photographs of candidates in the United States and Taiwan. *Asian Journal of Communication*, *4*(2), 121–129.

Lei, Cecilia. (2018). Majority of Black Americans Value Social Media For Amplifying Lesser-Known Issues. Retrieved from https://www.npr.org/2018/08/05/635127389/majority-of-black-americans-value-social-media-for-amplifying-lesser-known-issue

Leo, J. (2005). Reporters' feelings shape the news. *Tampa Bay Times*. Retrieved from https://www.tampabay.com/archive/1997/05/03/reporters-feelings-shape-the-news/

Leopold, J., & Bell, M. P. (2017). News media and the racialization of protest: An analysis of Black Lives Matter articles. *Equality, Diversity and Inclusion: An International Journal*, *36*(8), 720–735.

Levendowski, A. (2018). How copyright law can fix artificial intelligence's implicit bias problem. *Washington Law Review, 93*(2), 579–630. Retrieved from http://proxyhu.wrlc.org/login?url=https://search-proquest-com.proxyhu.wrlc.org/docview/2214888330?accountid=11490

Levy, S. (2012). Can an Algorithm Write a Better News Story than a Human Reporter? *Wired online, 4,* 12. Retrieved from https://www.wired.com/2012/04/can-an-algorithm-write-a-better-news-story-than-a-human-reporter/

Lewis, S., Sanders, A. K., Carmody, C. (Spring, 2019). Libel by Algorithm? Automated journalism and the Threat of Legal Liability. *Journalism & Mass Communication Quarterly*, *96*(1), 60–79.

Lincoln, Y. S., & Guba, E. G. (1985). *Naturalistic inquiry* (Vol. 75). Sage.

Lippmann, W. (2017). *Public opinion*. London, United Kingdom: Routledge.

Lippmann, W. (1922). The world outside and the pictures in our heads.

Little, T. D., Rhemtulla, M., Gibson, K., & Schoemann, A. M. (2013). Why the items versus parcels controversy needn't be one. *Psychological Methods*, *18*(3), 285.

Liyanagunawardena, T. R., Adams, A. A., & Williams, S. A. (2013). MOOCs: A systematic study of the published literature 2008-2012. *The International Review of Research in Open and Distributed Learning, 14*(3), 202–227.

Lockyer, S. (2004). Coding qualitative data. *The Sage Encyclopedia of Social Science Research Methods, 1*(1), 137–138.

Lombard, M., Snyder-Duch, J., & Bracken, C. C. (2004). Practical resources for assessing and reporting intercoder reliability in content analysis research projects. Retrieved on September 4, 2011, from http://astro.temple.edu/~lombard/reliability/.

Love, D. (2016). 2016 Nielsen Report: Black Buying Power Has Reached Tipping Point, But How Will Black America Leverage it to Create Wealth? Retrieved from https://atlantablackstar.com/2016/02/04/2016-nielsen-report-black-buying-power-reached-tipping-point-will-black-america-leverage-create-wealth/

Lu, K. (2017). Blacks more likely to follow up on digital news than whites. Retrieved from http://www.pewresearch.org/fact-tank/2017/03/02/blacks-more-likely-to-follow-up-on-digital-news-than-whites/

Lundman, R. J. (2003, September). The newsworthiness and selection bias in news about murder: Comparative and relative effects of novelty and race and gender typifications on newspaper coverage of homicide. In *Sociological forum* (Vol. 18, pp. 357–386). Kluwer Academic Publishers-Plenum Publishers.

Lyall, S. & Fausset, R. (2018, Oct. 26). Stacey Abrams, a Daughter of the South, Asks Georgia to Change. *New York Times*. Retrieved from https://www.nytimes.com/2018/10/26/us/politics/stacey-abrams-georgia-governor.html

Lynn, E. & Kennedy, M. (2018). NBC Cancels Megyn Kelly's Show After Blackface Controversy. *Afro.com*. Retrieved from https://afro.com/nbc-cancels-megyn-kellys-show-after-blackface-controversy/

Machina, M. (1990) Choice under uncertainty. Problems solved and unsolved. In K.S. Cook & M. Levi (Eds), *The Limits of Rationality,* (p. 90–132). Chicago: The University of Chicago Press.

Mackey, A., & Gass, S. M. (2005). *Second language research: Methodology and design*. Mahwah, NJ: Lawrence Erlbaum Associates.

MacKuen, M. B., & Coombs, S. L. (1981). More than news: Media power in public affairs. *(No Title)*.

Marconi, F., & Siegman, A., & Machine Journalist. (2017). The future of augmented journalism: A guide for newsrooms in the age of smart machines. Associated Press. Retrieved from https://insights ap.org/uploads/images/the-future-of-augmented-journalism_ap-report.pdf

Markides, C. (2010). Crossing the chasm: How to convert relevant research into managerially useful research. *The Journal of Applied Behavioral Science,* 0021886310388162.

Marris, S. (2018). Former VP Joe Biden calls for US midterm voters to reject division. Retrieved from https://news.sky.com/story/former-vp-joe-biden-calls-for-voters-to-reject-division-11544466

Marshall, S. (2013). Robot reporters: A look at the computers writing the news. *Journalism.co.uk, 12*.

Mazzei, (2018). Text Messages Raise New Questions Over Andrew Gillum's Lob-byist Connections. *The New York Times*. Retrieved from https://www.nytimes.com /2018/10/23/us/adam-corey-florida-governor-gillum.html

McChesney, R. W. (2015). The personal is political: The political economy of non-commercial radio broadcasting in the United States. *Monthly Review*, *66*(10), 47.

McChesney, R. W. (2004). *The problem of the media*. Alternative Radio. New York, NY: Monthly Review Press.

McCombs, M. (2018). *Setting the agenda: Mass media and public opinion*. John Wiley & Sons.

McCombs, M. (2005). A look at agenda-setting: Past, present, and future. Journalism Studies, 6 (4), 543–557.

McCombs, M. E. (2004). Setting the agenda: the mass media and public opinion. Malden, MA: Blackwell Publishing, Inc.

McCombs, M. (2002, June). The agenda-setting role of the mass media in the shaping of public opinion. In *Mass Media Economics 2002 Conference, London School of Economics: http://sticerd. lse. ac. uk/dps/extra/McCombs. pdf.*

McCombs, M. (1997). Building consensus: The news media's agenda-setting roles. *Political communication, 14*(4), 433–443.

McCombs, M. E. (1992). Explorers and surveyors: Expanding strategies for agenda-setting research. *Journalism quarterly, 69*(4), 813–824.

McCombs, M. E. (1972). Mass Communication in Political Campaigns: Information, Gratification and Persuasion. In F. Kline, & J. Tichenor (Eds.), Current Perspectives in Mass Communication Research. Beverly Hills, CA: Sage.

McCombs, M., Llamas, J. P., Lopez-Escobar, E., & Rey, F. (1997). Candidate images in Spanish elections: Second-level agenda-setting effects. *Journalism & Mass Communication Quarterly, 74*(4), 703–717.

McCombs, M.E., & Shaw, D.L. (1993). The evolution of agenda-setting research: Twenty-five years in the marketplace. Journal of Communication. 43(2). 58–67.

McCombs, M. E., & Shaw, D. L. (1972). The agenda-setting function of mass media. The Public Opinion Quarterly, 36 (2), 176–187.

McCombs, M. E., Shaw, D. L., & Weaver, D. H. (Eds.). (2013). *Communication and democracy: Exploring the intellectual frontiers in agenda-setting theory*. Routledge.

McIlwain, C. D. (2011). Racialized Media Coverage of Minority Candidates in the 2008 Democratic Presidential Primary. *American Behavioral Scientist, 55*(4), 371–389. https://doi.org/10.1177/0002764211398067

McLeod, D. M. (2007). News coverage and social protest: How the media's protect paradigm exacerbates social conflict. *J. Disp. Resol.*, 185.

McLeod, J. M. (1987). Audience Perspectives on the News: Assessing Their Complexity and Conceptual Frames.

McLeod, D. M., and Detenber, B. (1999). Framing Effects of Television News Coverage of Social Protest. *Journal of Communication (49)*3, p. 3–23.

McLuhan, M., & Fiore, Q. (1967). The medium is the message. *New York, 123*, 126–128.

McQuail, D. (2010). *McQuail's mass communication theory*. Sage publications.

McQuail, D. (2008). *McQuail's Mass Communication Theory* (5 ed.). London: Sage Publications Ltd.

McQuail, D. (1994). *Mass communication theory. An introduction.* Denis McQuail.

Melican, D. B., & Dixon, T. L. (2008). News on the net: Credibility, selective exposure, and racial prejudice. *Communication Research, 35*(2), 151–168.

Mellinger, G. (2017). The Riot Report and the News: How the Kerner Commission Changed Media Coverage of Black America. *Journalism History, 42*(4), 240.

Mendelsohn, M. (1993). Television's frames in the 1988 Canadian election. *Canadian journal of communication, 18*(2).

Mensing, D. (2017). The curious case of US journalism education: Shrinking newsrooms, expanding classrooms. *Global journalism education in the 21st century: Challenges & innovations*, 219–242.

Milbank, D. (2001). *Smashmouth: Notes from the 2000 campaign trail.* New York: Basic Books.

Miles, Hugh. (2005). *Al-Jazeera: How Arab TV challenges America.* Great Britain: Abacus.

Montal, T., & Reich, Z. (2017). I, robot. You, journalist. Who is the author? Authorship, bylines and full disclosure in automated journalism. *Digital Journalism, 5*(7), 829–849.

Monti, M. (2019). Automated Journalism and Freedom of Information: Ethical and Juridical Problems Related to AI in the Press Field. *Opinio Juris in Comparatione, 1.*

Morgan, V. (2018, Nov. 5). It took years for African-Americans to have a voice. Shame on us if we don't vote. *Courier Journal: Part of the USA Today Network.* https://www.courier-journal.com/story/opinion/2018/11/05/elections-2018-they-fought-bled-and-died-so-we-could-vote/1839235002/

Morgan-Smith, K. (2018). Bank exec slammed for dressing as Kanye in blackface with MAGA hat. *TheGrio.com.* Retrieved from https://thegrio.com/2018/10/30/bank-exec-slammed-for-dressing-as-kanye-in-blackface-with-maga-hat/

Morris, M., & Ogan, C. (1996). The internet as mass medium. *Journal of Communication. 46*(1), pages 39–50, March 1996 doi: 10.1111/j.14602466.1996.tb01460.x

Morton, V. (2018, October, 28). Candace Owens pushes "Blexit" campaign: "No group . . . more taken advantage of by the Democrats.". *The Washington Times,* Retrieved from https://www.washingtontimes.com/news/2018/oct/28/candace-owens-pushes-blexit-ahead-midterm-election/

Moses, L. (2017). *The Washington Post's* robot reporter has published 850 articles in the past year. Retrieved from https://digiday.com/media/washington-posts-robot-reporter-published-500-articles-last-year/

Morton, V. (2018). (October 23, 2018). Ga. governor hopeful Stacey Abrams admits she burned state flag at protest. *The Washington Times.* Retrieved from https://www.washingtontimes.com/news/2018/oct/22/stacey-abrams-admits-she-burned-georgia-state-flag/

NABJ Commemorates 50th Anniversary of the Kerner Commission Report. (2018). Retrieved from https://www.nabj.org/news/388966/NABJ-Commemorates-50th-Anniversary-of-the-Kerner-Commission-Report-.htm

The Nation's Top 100 Newspapers. (2018). The Nation's Top 100 Newspapers. Retrieved from nyjobsource.com/papers.html

Neuendorf, K. A. (2016). *The content analysis guidebook.* Thousand Oaks, CA: Sage Publications.

Neuendorf, A. (2002). *The content analysis guidebook.* Thousand Oaks, CA: Sage Publications.

NewMedia Wire. (2023). World's First AI-Generated News Channel Launches-NewsGPT. Retrieved from https://finance.yahoo.com/news/worlds-first-ai-generated-news-224448989.html?soc_src=social-sh&soc_trk=ma

Noble, S. U. (2018). *Algorithms of Oppression: How search engines reinforce racism.* NYU Press.

Norvig, P. (2012). Artificial intelligence: Early ambitions. *New Scientist, 216*(2889), ii–iii.

Noelle-Neuman, E. & Mathes, R. (1987). The event as event and the event as news: The significance of consonance for media effects research. *European Journal of Communication,* 2, 391–414.

Noelle-Neumann, E. (1973). Return to the concept of powerful mass media. *Studies of Broadcasting,* 9, 67–112.

Nowell, L. S., Norris, J. M., White, D. E., & Moules, N. J. (2017). Thematic analysis: Striving to meet the trustworthiness criteria. *International Journal of Qualitative Methods, 16*(1), 1609406917733847.

News consumption patterns among African Americans and Hispanics. (2014). Retrieved from https://www.americanpressinstitute.org/publications/reports/survey-research/news-consumption-patterns-african-americans-hispanics/

Oliver, M. B. (2003). African American men as "criminal and dangerous": Implications of media portrayals of crime on the "criminalization" of African American men. *Journal of African American Studies,* 3–18.

Onwuegbuzie, A. J., & Leech, N. L. (2007). Sampling designs in qualitative research: Making the sampling process more public. *The Qualitative Report, 12*(2), 238–254.

Onwumechili, C. (2017). Introduction to the Special Issue on the Barack Hussein Obama Presidency. *Howard Journal of Communications, 28*(1), 1–5.

Onwumechili, C. (2017). *Sport communication: An international approach.* Retrieved from https://search-proquest-com.proxyhu.wrlc.org/legacydocview/EBC/4980508?accountid=11490.com

Ormston, R., Spencer, L., Barnard, M., & Snape, D. (2014). The foundations of qualitative research. Qualitative research practice. A guide for social science students and researchers, 1–25.

Owens, D. (2018). Reaching Millennials and Young Voters with Education, Entertainment. *TheGrio.com.* Retrieved from https://thegrio.com/2018/10/30/reaching-millennials-and-young-voters-with-education-entertainment/

Palmer, G., d'Orazio, V., Kenwick, M., & Lane, M. (2015). The MID4 dataset, 2002–2010: Procedures, coding rules and description. *Conflict Management and Peace Science, 32*(2), 222–242.

Pan, Z., & Kosicki, G. M. (1993). Framing analysis: An approach to news discourse. *Political Communication, 10*(1), 55–75.

Park, S., Holody, K. J., & Zhang, X. (2012). Race in media coverage of school shootings: A parallel application of framing theory and attribute agenda-setting. *Journalism and Mass Communication Quarterly, 89*(3), 475–494. Retrieved from http://proxyhu.wrlc.org/login?url=https://search-proquest-com.proxyhu.wrlc.org/docview/1036601499?accountid=11490

Paton, D., & McClure, J. (2013). Hazard preparedness: Community engagement and empowerment. In *Preparing for disaster: Building household and community capacity* (p. 143–152). Springfield, IL: Charles C. Thomas.

Patterson, A. M. (1993). *Reading between the Lines*. Univ of Wisconsin Press.

Patton, M. Q. (1999). Enhancing the quality and credibility of qualitative analysis. *Health Services Research, 34*(5 Pt 2), 1189.

Patton, M. Q. (1990). *Qualitative evaluation and research methods*. SagePublications, Inc.

Pederson, R., Kalita, B., & Burke, K. (2022). Machine learning and density functional theory. *Nature Reviews Physics, 4*(6), 357–358.

Perkins, D. J., & Starosta, W. J. (2001). Representing coculturals: On form and news portrayals of Native Americans. *Howard Journal of Communication, 12*(2), 73–84.

Perreault, W. D., & Leigh, L. E. (1989). Reliability of nominal data based on qualitative judgements. *Journal of Marketing Research, 26*, 135–148.

Piketty, T. (2015). About capital in the twenty-first century. *American Economic Review, 105*(5), 48–53.

Pingree, R. J., & Stoycheff, E. (2013). Differentiating cueing from reasoning in agenda-setting effects. *Journal of Communication, 63*(5), 852–872.

Poggenpoel, M., & Myburgh, C. (2003). The researcher as research instrument in educational research: A possible threat to trustworthiness? *Education, 124*(2),418–421. Retrieved from https://eds-b-ebscohost-com.ezwaldenulibrary .org/eds/pdfviewer/pdfviewer?vid=2&sid=0abee29d- 98d2-426c-960f-3fecb0f2b3 91%40sessionmgr102

Pole, A. (2010). *Blogging the political: Politics and participation in a Networked Society*. New York: Routledge.

Pole, A. (2005). Black bloggers and the blogosphere, paper presented at the Second International Conference on Technology, Knowledge, and Society, Hyderbad, India. Retrieved from http://www.mdcbowen.org/cobb/archives/pole_black_bloggers.pdf.

Polit, D. F., & Beck, C. T. (2012). *Nursing research: Generating and assessing evidence for nursing practices*. Philadelphia, PA: Lippincott Williams and Wilkins.

Pool, I. (1983). *Technologies of freedom*. Cambridge, MA: Belknap Press.

Popescu, Gheorghe H. (2017). "Is Lying Acceptable Conduct in International Politics?," *Educational Philosophy and Theory, 49*(6): 575–576.

Porterfield, J. (2016). *White and black hat hackers* (37). The Rosen Publishing Group, Inc.

Powers, K. (2018, October 25). Megyn Kelly was making racist comments long before "blackface." NBC hired her anyway. USAToday.com. Retrieved from https://www.usatoday.com/story/opinion/2018/10/25/megyn-kelly-nbc-blackface -racist-comments-white-supremacy-column/1760679002/

Price, V., Tewksbury, D., (1995). News values and public opinion: A theoretical account of media priming and framing. Paper presented at the annual conference of the International Communication Association, Albuquerque, NM.

Price, V., Tewksbury, D., & Powers, E. (1997). Switching trains of thought: The impact of news frames on readers'' cognitive responses. *Communication research*, 24(5), 481–506.

Pride, A. S., & Wilson, C. C. (1997). *A history of the Black press* (12). Washington, DC: Howard University Press.

Prince, R. (2018). Technology Is Building a Future Without People of Color in Mind. Retrieved from https://journalisms.theroot.com/technology-is-building-a-future-without-people-of-color-1823314135

Prince, Richard. (2018). The Root Closes In on BET.com: Two Top the List of Most-Viewed Black Websites. Retrieved from journal-isms.com/2018/08/howard-u-mentor-to-stay-on-campus/?fbclid=IwAR3jNXf3uwwWjmneSRjYG3d2nj BtTffkKt9OpJztYUrtRjPGoUpFiEQ9lTc#The%20Root%20Closes%20In%20on %20BET.com

Rahman, Abid. (2020). CES 2020: Artificial Intelligence Takes Center Stage. Retrieved from: https://www.intouchg.com/blog/artificial-intelligence/ces-2020 -artificial-intelligence-takes-center-stage/

Ramasubramanian, S., & Martinez, A. R. (2017). News framing of Obama, racialized scrutiny, and symbolic racism. Howard Journal of Communications, 28(1), 36–54.

Reese, S.D. (2001). Prologue—Framing public life: A bridging model for media research. In S.D. Reese, O.H. Gandy, Jr., & A.E. Grant (Eds.), Framing public life: Perspectives on media and our understanding of the social world (p 7–31). New York, NY: Routledge.

Reese, S.D. (2010). Finding frames in a web of culture: The case of the war on terror. In D'Angelo & J.A. Kuypers (Eds.), Doing news framing analysis: Empirical and theoretical perspectives (p 17–42). New York, NY: Routledge.

Reid, M. (1993). Redefining Black film. Berkeley: University of California Press.

Report of the National Advisory Commission on Civil Disorders. (1968). [Washington: United States, Kerner Commission: U.S. G.P.O.

Riffe, D., Lacy, S., & Fico, F. G. (1998). Analyzing media messages: Using quantitative content analysis in research. Mahwah, NJ: Lawrence Erlbaum Associates, Inc.

Rikap, C., Lundvall, B. Å., Rikap, C., & Lundvall, B. Å. (2021). AI policies and politics in China and the US between techno-globalism and techno-nationalism. *The Digital Innovation Race: Conceptualizing the Emerging New World Order*, 145-163.

Robinson, C. & Cantey, N. (2016). Out or In? The black blogosphere And the News Media. *Glocalism: Journal of Culture, 2016*(1), Glocalism: Journal of Culture, 01 May 2016, Vol.2016(1).

Rogers, E. M., Dearing, J. W., & Bregman, D. (1993). The anatomy of agenda-setting research. *Journal of communication*, 43(2), 68–84.

Roth, S., Tuch, A. N., Mekler, E. D., Bargas-Avila, J. A., & Opwis, K. (2013). Location matters, especially for non-salient features–An eye-tracking study on the effects of web object placement on different types of websites. *International journal of human-computer studies, 71*(3), 228–235.

The Royal Society. (2018). Portrayals and perceptions of AI and why they matter. Retrieved from https://royalsociety.org/~/media/policy/projects/ai-narratives/AI-narratives-workshop-findings.pdf

Rubaai, A., Ricketts, D., & Kankam, M. D. (2002). Development and implementation of an adaptive fuzzy-neural-network controller for brushless drives. *IEEE Transactions on Industry Applications, 38*(2), 441–447.

Ruiz, M. (2018). Megyn Kelly Apologizes For Asking "What Is Racist" About Blackface. Vogue. Retrieved from https://www.vogue.com/article/megyn-kelly-blackface-halloween-what-is-racist

Russell, S. J., & Norvig, (2016). *Artificial intelligence: a modern approach*. Malaysia; Pearson Education Limited,.

Saldaña, J. (2015). The coding manual for qualitative researchers. Sage.

Salwen, M. B., & Matera, F. R. (1992). Public salience of foreign nations. Journalism Quarterly, 69 (3), 623–632.

Sanchez, D. (2017). *Artificial Intelligence Is Inheriting Human Bias. Here's Why Diversity and Inclusion Matter*. The Moguldom Nation. Retrieved from https://moguldom.com/7529/artificial-intelligence-ai-is-inheriting-human-bias-why-diversity-and-inclusion-matter/

Scheufele, D. A. (2000). Agenda-setting, priming, and framing revisited: Another look at cognitive effects of political communication. *Mass communication and society, 3*(2–3), 297–316.

Scheufele, D. A. (1999). Framing as a theory of media effects. Journal of communication, 49(1), 103–122.

Scheufele, D. A., & Tewksbury, D. (2009). News framing theory and research. In Media effects (p 33–49). Routledge.

Scheufele, B. (2004). Framing-effects approach: A theoretical and methodological critique. Communications, 29(4), 401–428.

Schreier, M. (2014). Qualitative content analysis. The Sage handbook of qualitative data analysis, 170–183.

Seager, S. (2017). No, It's Not Fake News, It's Robot-Written News: Google funds reporter robots in Europe, part of a growing trend. *TheWrap*. Retrieved from https://www.thewrap.com/no-its-not-fake-news-its-robot-written-news/

Shah, A. (2012). Mainstream Media Introduction. Retrieved from www.globalissues.org/article/278/mainstream-media-introduction

Shearer, E., & Grieco, E. (2019). Americans are wary of the role social media sites play in delivering the news. *Pew Research Center, 2.*

Shenton, A. K. (2004). Strategies for ensuring trustworthiness in qualitative research projects. Education for Information, 22(2), 63–75. https://dx.doi.org/10.3233/EFI2004-22201

SimilarWeb.com. (2023). Website Analysis: theroot.com. Retrieved from https://pro.similarweb.com/#/digitalsuite/websiteanalysis/overview/website-performance/*/999/3m?webSource=Total&key=theroot.com

Skoric, M. M., & Park, Y. J. (2014). Culture, technologies and democracy: A cross-national analysis of political development. *Telematics and Informatics, 31*(3), 364–375.

Slater, M. D. (2007). Reinforcing spirals: The mutual influence of media selectivity and media effects and their impact on individual behavior and social identity. *Communication theory, 17*(3), 281–303.

Smiley, C., & Fakunle, D. (2016). From "brute" to "thug:" The demonization and criminalization of unarmed Black male victims in America. Journal of human behavior in the social environment, 26(3–4), 350–366.

Solas, M. (2018). Black Women Candidates Running in 2018 Face More Obstacle, Political Experts Say. Newsweek.com Retrieved from https://www.newsweek.com /black-women-candidates-running-2018-face-more-obstacles-political-experts-say -877825

Spencer, T. & Farrington, B. (2018). Gillum, DeSantis Exchange Insults in Final Florida Debate. *Afro.com.* Retrieved from https://afro.com/gillum-desantis-exchange -insults-in-final-florida-debate/

Squires, C. (2002). Rethinking the Black Public Sphere: An Alternative Vocabulary for Multiple Public Spheres. *Communication Theory, 12*(4), 446–468.

Sripada, S., Reiter, E., and Davy, I. (2003). SumTime-Mousam: Configurable marine weather forecast generator. *Expert Update*, 6(3):4–10.

Starr, T. J. (2018, October 23). Black College Students in Florida Use Early Voting to Make Sure Their Voices Will Be Taken Seriously. TheRoot.com. Retrieved from https://www.theroot.com/black-college-students-in-florida-use-early-voting-to-m -1829937174

Sterling, Christopher H. (2009). "Electronic News Gathering". Encyclopedia of Journalism. 2: 504.

Stirling, A. (2007). A general framework for analyzing diversity in science, technology and society. Journal of The Royal Society Interface, 4(15), 707–719. Retrieved from https://doi.org/10.1098/rsif.2007.0213

Strömbäck J (2005) In search of a standard: Four models of democracy and their normative implications for journalism. Journalism Studies 6(3): 331–345.

Sanders, M. S., & Sullivan, J. M. (2010). Category inclusion and exclusion in perceptions of African Americans: using the stereotype content model to examine perceptions of groups and individuals. *Race, Gender & Class, 17*(3), 201-212,214-222. Retrieved from http://proxyhu.wrlc.org/login?url=https://search-proquest-com .proxyhu.wrlc.org/docview/762223636?accountid=11490

Sun, F. (2022). ChatGPT, the Start of a New Era.

Sutton, J., & Austin, Z. (2015). Qualitative research: Data collection, analysis, and management. The Canadian Journal of Hospital Pharmacy, 68(3), 226-231. Retrieved from https://www.ncbi.nlm.nih.gov/pmc/articles/PMC4485510/

Tankard, J. (2001). The empirical approach to the study of media framing. In S. Reese, O. Gandy, Jr., & A.E. Grant (Eds.), *Framing public life* (p 95–106). Mahwah, NJ: Lawrence Erlbaum.

Tankard, J.W. (1997). PR goes to war: The effects of public relations campaigns on media framing of the Kuwaiti and Bosnian crises. Presented at Association for Education in Journalism and Mass Communication (AEJMC), Chicago.

Tankard, J., Hendrickson, L. Silberman, J. Bliss, K., & Ghanem, S. (1991, August). Media Frames: Approaches to Conceptualization and Measurement. Paper presented AEJMC, Boston, MA.

Telusma, B. (2018, November 2). Black doctor claims she was racially profiled on a Delta flight to Boston. TheGrio.com. Retrieved from https://thegrio.com/2018/11/02/black-doctor-claims-delta-racially-profiled/

Tharps, L. (2013). Do we still need a black media? A vibrant black media and a more inclusive mainstream media should both be available to the public. Retrieved from https://archives.cjr.org/minority_reports/black_media_separate_and_equal.php

TheGrio.com. (2023). About TheGrio. *TheGrio.com*. Retrieved from https://thegrio.com/about/

TheGrio. (2018). The Grio's 2018 Midterm Election Blog: What Black America Needs to Know. TheGrio. Retrieved from https://thegrio.com/2018/11/06/thegrios-2018-midterm-election-blog/

The Root Staff. (2016). Advertise on The Root. TheRoot.com. Retrieved from https://www.theroot.com/advertise-on-the-root-1790854632

Thibodeaux, J. (2016). City racial composition as a predictor of African American food deserts. *Urban Studies, 53*(11), 2238–2252. Retrieved from doi:http://dx.doi.org.proxyhu.wrlc.org/10.1177/0042098015587848

Thurman, N. (2018). Newspaper consumption in the mobile age. *Journalism Studies, 19*(10), 1409–1429. doi:http://dx.doi.org.proxy.bc.edu/10.1080/1461670X.2017.1279028

Thurman, Dörr, and Kunert. (2017). When Reporters Get Hands-on with Robo-Writing, Digital Journalism, 5:10, 1240-1259, DOI: 10.1080/21670811.2017.1289819

Tiffen ,R. (1988). Politicians' experiences with the news: Insight from the Howson diaries. Media Information Australia, 49, 25–29.

Toma, J. D. (2014). Approaching rigor in applied qualitative research. In *The Sage handbook for research in education: Pursuing ideas as the keystone of exemplary inquiry* (2nd ed. (p 405–423). Thousand Oaks, CA: Sage.

Tracy, J. (2017). News media offers consistently warped portrayals of black families, study finds. Retrieved from https://www.washingtonpost.com/news/wonk/wp/2017/12/13/news-media-offers-consistently-warped-portrayals-of-black-families-study-finds/?utm_term=.e54f69efe93d

Trammell, K. D., & Gasser, U. (2004). Deconstructing weblogs: An analytical framework for analyzing online journals. Paper presented at the International Communication Association, New Orleans, LA.

Tuchman, G. (1978). Introduction: The symbolic annihilation of women by the mass media. In G. Tuckman, A.K. Daniels, J. Benet (Eds.), Hearth and home: Images of women in the mass media. New York: Oxford University.

Tuchman, G. (1978). Making news: A study in the construction of reality. New York: Free Press.

Tucker, C. (2017). Privacy, Algorithms and Artificial Intelligence. Retrieved from https://www.nber.org/chapters/c14011.pdf

Tukachinsky, R. (2017). Media Portrayals and Effects: African Americans. In *Oxford Research Encyclopedia of Communication*.

Twenge, J. M., Martin, G.N., & Spitzberg, B. H. (2019). Trends in US Adolescents' media use,1976–2016: The rise of digital media, the decline of TV, and the (near) demiseof print. *Psychology of Popular Media Culture, 8*(4),329.

Twomey, J. L. (2001). Newspaper Coverage of the 1992 Los Angeles Uprising: Race, Place, and the Story of the" Riot": Racial Ideology in African American and Korean American Newspapers. *Race, Gender & Class*, 140–154.

Tversky, A., Slovic, & Kahneman, D. (1990). The causes of preference reversal. *The American Economic Review*, 204–217.

Tversky, A., & Kahneman, D. (1986). Rational choice and the framing of decisions. *Journal of business*, S251–S278.

Ulanoff, Lance. (2014). "Need to Write 5 Million Stories a Week? Robot Reporters to the Rescue." Retrieved from https://mashable.com/2014/07/01/robot-reporters-add-data-to-the-five-ws/#5Y5NVqQ0igqj

Underwood, T. (2019). *Distant horizons: digital evidence and literary change*. University of Chicago Press.

United States. National Advisory Council on Economic Opportunity. (1967). *Annual Report-National Advisory Council on Economic Opportunity*. US Government Printing Office.

Vaismoradi, M., Turunen, H. & Bondas, T. (2013). Content analysis and thematic analysis: Implications for conducting a qualitative descriptive study. Nursing and Health Sciences, 15(3), 398–405.

Van der Haak, B., Parks, M., & Castells, M. (2012). The future of journalism: Networked journalism. *International journal of communication, 6*, 16.

Van Dijk, T. A. (1993). Principles of critical discourse analysis. Discourse & society, 4(2), 249283.

Vandiver, B. J., Fhagen-Smith, Cokley, K. O., Cross, William E., Jr, & Worrell, F. C. (2001). Cross's nigrescence model: From theory to scale to theory. *Journal of Multicultural Counseling and Development, 29*(3), 174. Retrieved from http://proxyhu.wrlc.org/login?url=https://search-proquest-com.proxyhu.wrlc.org/docview/235920717?accountid=11490

Van Drehle, David. (2000, August 2). Spectators at son's rise. The Washington Post. Retrieved August 2,2000, from the World Wide Web: http://www.washingtonpost.com /wp-dyn/politics

Varney, J. (2018). Andrew Gillum still holds lead in Florida's gubernatorial race, poll shows. *The Washington Times*. Retrieved from https://www.washingtontimes.com/news/2018/oct/23/andrew-gillum-still-holds-lead-floridas-gubernator/

Varney, James. (November 6, 2018). Michigan paper fires reporter for bias against GOP Senate candidate John James. *The Washington Times*. Retrieved from https://www.washingtontimes.com/news/2018/nov/6/michigan-paper-fires-reporter-bias-against-gop-sen/

Viswanath, K., & Arora, P. (2000). Ethnic media in the United States: An essay on their role in integration, assimilation, and social control. *Mass Communication & Society, 3*(1), 39–56.

Waddell, T. (Spring, 2019). Can an algorithm reduce the perceived bias of news? Testing the effect of machine attribution on news readers' evaluations of bias, anthropomorphism, and credibility. *Journalism & Mass Communication Quarterly, 96*(1), 82–100.

Wallsten, K. (2007). Agenda-setting and the blogosphere: An analysis of the relationship between mainstream media and political blogs. *Review of Policy Research, 24*(6), 567–587.

Wang, W. (2011). *A content analysis of reliability in advertising content analysis studies* (Order No. 1507476). Available from ABI/INFORM Global; ProQuest Dissertations & Theses Global. (918226545). Retrieved from http://proxyhu.wrlc .org/login?url=https://search-proquest-com.proxyhu.wrlc.org/docview/918226545 ?accountid=11490

Wanta, W., Williams, J. & Hu, Y. (1993). The Agenda-setting effects of international news coverage: An examination of differing news frames. *International Journal of Public Opinion Research, 5*, 250–264.

WashPostPR. (2018). The Post's Heliograf and ModBot technologies take first place in 2018 Global BIGGIES Awards. Retrieved from https://www.washingtonpost .com/pr/wp/2018/03/23/the-posts-heliograf-and-modbot-technologies-take-first -place-in-2018-global-biggies-awards/?utm_term=.18fc34ad0d97

Wasserman, H. (2006). Tackles and sidesteps: Normative maintenance and paradigm repair in mainstream reactions to South African tabloid journalism. *Communicare: Journal for Communication Sciences in Southern Africa, 25*(1), 59–80.

Watson, A. (2019). Statista. Retrieved from https://www.statista.com/statistics /273503/average-paid-weekday-circulation-of-the-new-york-times/

Weaver, D. H. (2007). Thoughts on agenda-setting, framing, and priming. *Journal of Communication, 57*(1), 142–147.

Weaver, D., Graber, D. McCombs, M., & Eyal C. (1981). *Media agenda-setting in a presidential election: Issues, images and interests.* New York: Praeger.

Webb, A. (2016). *The signals are talking: why today's fringe is tomorrow's mainstream.* PublicAffairs.

Weeks, B. (2014). Safe Harbor and Copyright Infringement on the Internet: A Need to Update the Paradigm. *RJSH, 33.*

Welch, K. (2007). Black Criminal Stereotypes and Racial Profiling. *Journal of Contemporary Criminal Justice, 23*(3), 276–288. Retrieved from https://doi.org/10 .1177/1043986207306870

The White House. (2022). Blueprint for an AI Bill of Rights. Retrieved from https:// www.whitehouse.gov/ostp/ai-bill-of-rights/.

Wilson II, C. C., Gutierrez, F., & Chao, L. (2012). *Racism, sexism, and the media: Multicultural issues into the new communications age.* Sage Publications.

Wilson, W. J. (2009). Framing race and poverty. *Contexts, 8*(4), 84. doi:http://dx.doi. org.proxyhu.wrlc.org/10.1525/ctx.2009.8.4.84

Wilson, C. (2008, Apr 03). Another day of infamy: MLK, Jr. assassinated April 4, 1968. *Precinct Reporter*. Retrieved from http://proxyhu.wrlc.org/login?url=https://search-proquest-com.proxyhu.wrlc.org/docview/367803451?accountid=11490

Wilson, C. C., Gutierrez, F., and Chao, L. M. (2003). *Racism, sexism and the media the rise of class communication in multicultural America* (3rd ed), 116. Thousand Oaks, CA: Sage Publications.

Wilson, C. C., & Gutierrez, F. (1985). *Minorities and the Media*. Beverly Hills, CA, London: Sage.

Windey, B., & Cleeremans, A. (2015). Consciousness as a graded and an all-or none phenomenon: A conceptual analysis. *Consciousness and Cognition*, 35, 185–191.

Wingfield, A. H. & Feagin, J. (2012). "The racial dialectic: President Barack Obama and the white racial frame." *Qualitative Sociology* 35 (2012): 143–162.

Winter, J., & Eyal C. (1981). Agenda-setting for the Civil Rights issue. *Public Opinion Quarterly*, 45, 376–383.

Wintonick, P. (1994). *Manufacturing consent: Noam Chomsky and the media: the companion book to the award-winning film by Peter Wintonick and Mark Achbar* (Vol. 207). Black Rose Books Ltd.

Wlezien, C. (2003). Presidential election polls in 2000: A study in dynamics. *Presidential Studies Quarterly*, *33*(1), 172–186.

Wölker, A., & Powell, T. E. (2018). Algorithms in the newsroom? News readers' perceived credibility and selection of automated journalism. *Journalism*. https://doi.org/10.1177/1464884918757072

Wrench, J. S., Thomas-Maddox, C., Richmond, V., & McCroskey, J. C. (2008). *Quantitative Research Methods for Communication*. New York, NY: Oxford University Press.

Xue, Y., Liu, Z., Gao, X., Jin, C., Wen, L., Yao, X., & Ren, J. (2010). GPS-SNO: computational prediction of protein S-nitrosylation sites with a modified GPS algorithm. *PloS one*, *5*(6), e11290.

Yagade, A., & Dozier, D. M. (1990). The media agenda-setting effect of concrete versus abstract issues. *Journalism Quarterly*, *67*(1), 3–10.

Yoes, S. (2018). Gillum Surges Ahead in Florida. *Afro.com*. Retrieved from https://afro.com/gillum-surges-ahead-in-florida/

Zahangir, K. (2019). Technological advancements in present-day journalism: Prospects and challenges. Financial Express. Retrieved from https://today.thefinancialexpress.com.bd/views-reviews/technological-advancements-in-present-day-journalism-prospects-and-challenges-1562938589?amp=true

Zhongdang Pan, & Kosicki, G. M. (1993). Framing Analysis: An Approach to News Discourse. *Political Communication*, *10*(1), 55–75. https://doiorg.dax.lib.unf.edu/10.1080/10584609.1993.9962963

Zhou, X. (2017). Management Strategy for China's internet Media Industry.

Zillmann, D., Gibson, R., & Sargent, S. L. (1999). Effects of photographs in news-magazine reports on issue perception. *Media Psychology*, *1*(3), 207–228. University Press.

Zucker, H. (1978). The variable nature of news media influence. In Brent Ruben (Ed.), *Communication Yearbook 2* (pp. 109–130). News Brunswick, NJ: Transaction.

Index

About the Author

Colin H. Campbell, PhD, is an award-winning communications scholar and doctoral graduate from Howard University's, Cathy Hughes School of Communications. Dr. Campbell's research focuses on the use of communications in media, technology, and policy. He was awarded as a 2023–2024 Frederick Douglass Institute Fellow at Shippensburg University and was inducted into the Edward Bouchet Graduate Honor Society at Yale University in 2020. Dr. Campbell's other research areas include news, journalism, media political economy, media production, equity, and cultural studies, where he analyzes systemic communications disparities that persist in American society pervading United States' polisocioeconomic structures. His professional academic experience includes teaching at several Washington, DC-metro area and Pennsylvania universities. Dr. Campbell created PanAfricanReport.com to bridge knowledge and cultural gaps among diverse populations descended from African diasporic countries. He is also a working television journalist for various international media outlets. He has covered the Biden, Trump, Obama, Bush, and Biden administrations, as well as Congress, the Occupy movement, and numerous US Department agencies. Dr. Campbell is the current president of the Capital Press Club and the immediate past-president of the Maryland Communication Association.